front of house

Oliver Heath with Nikki Blustin
Gardens by Lisa Buckland

CASSELL
ILLUSTRATED

Oliver and Nikki would like to offer a big thank you to Angela Huntbach for all her help, hard work and research with the writing of this book.

First published in Great Britain in 2005 by Cassell Illustrated
A division of Octopus Publishing Group
2–4 Heron Quays
London E14 4JP

A CIP catalogue record for this book is available from the British Library.

ISBN 1 84403 383 X
EAN 9781844033836

Book design by Smith & Gilmour

Printed in Italy by Printer Trento

CONTENTS

INTRODUCTION 6

CHAPTER 1
FIRST IMPRESSIONS COUNT 8

CHAPTER 2
GETTING STARTED 22

CHAPTER 3
ENTRANCES: DOORS AND PORCHES 36

CHAPTER 4
WINDOW OPENINGS AND ACCESSORIES 56

CHAPTER 5
WALLS AND BOUNDARIES 76

CHAPTER 6
LIGHTING BY DAY AND NIGHT 96

CHAPTER 7
HARD LANDSCAPING 114

CHAPTER 8
SOFT LANDSCAPING 134

RESOURCES 154
INDEX 158

INTRODUCTION

When I started thinking about *Front of House*, I wondered just how much scope there was to be creative, to find exciting, innovative design ideas that would really make a difference to the houses and streets of Britain.

Initially it seemed daunting, but once I got underway I was amazed at how many design opportunities exist, from a simple front-door makeover to totally revamping the design of the front of your house.

We are all aware that the way we dress, what we eat and how we decorate the insides of our homes says a lot about ourselves to others. Design has become an essential form of self-expression. It has allowed us to explore our creativity and not to simply go with what is handed down to us from generation to generation. It's about finding appropriate solutions for the way we want to live that will bring fun, function and individuality into our lives.

So why is it that we are still willing to accept that the way houses were designed and built 10, 20, 30, 40, even 100 years ago is still relevant to the way we live today? Why do we assume that we can't change the architecture around us and make a difference to our houses and our streets? Design has allowed us to become more self-expressive and to break the shackles of conventionality, making our houses look the way we want them to. I truly believe that it's time for a change, time for us to reclaim the fronts of our houses and be bold enough to say, 'This is who I am'.

Many people feel anxious about altering the front of their house in case it 'stands out' and doesn't fit in with the rest of the neighbourhood. This can be true if you live within an area of architectural value such as a Conservation Area, but in many cases the houses that we live in really have very little design merit. Just take a look around your neighbourhood. Ask yourself how many houses wouldn't benefit from a fresh coat of paint, a splash of colour, a more welcoming, better-lit front door, or a front garden that was a pleasure to be in and a benefit to the whole street? *Front of House* is all about helping you to find appropriate design solutions for you and your house.

In making this series it has been exciting to see houses being transformed – from dreary, pebbledashed façades and lifeless, rubbish-strewn gardens to vibrant areas that contain colour, plants, flowers, water features, welcoming front doors, and pathways and fences that define street space from home space. These houses have reclaimed their owners' sense of pride and revitalized whole neighbourhoods. It makes you realize just how much brighter and exciting the streetscapes of Britain could be if we all got involved and gave a touch of design inspiration to the fronts of our houses.

We have written this book not to tell you what to do to the front of your house, but to open your eyes to the possibilities that exist, from design concepts to materials, to lighting and landscaping. We want you to find ways to express yourselves – your style, your character, your passions – and to use these ideas to create a front of house that reflects who you are. We want you to enjoy your homes, and we want Britain to be a more exciting, colourful and creative place to live in.

So now it's up to you – just go for it!

CHAPTER 1
FIRST IMPRESSIONS COUNT

We are all familiar with the ideas that our home interiors say a lot about us, and that first impressions matter. But why are these first impressions not created at the front of our houses? Why do we feel that the exterior of our houses are fixed and cannot be touched or altered in a way that reflects who we are and our characters? It really is a missed opportunity. Consider afresh what it feels like to arrive at your front door. What does the front of your house say about you and your neighbourhood? Think about the way it looks, the way it smells, the way it sounds and how it feels. The options open to you are virtually unlimited, so it's time to do something about the front of your house.

INTRODUCTION

Britain is a nation of home-lovers, and while the phrase 'an Englishman's home is his castle' may now seem rather politically incorrect, it reminds us that we have always been a nation for whom our homes have been special.

A successful entrance and a good first impression can be created by considering colour, materials, textures, planting and lighting.

So why is it that compared with the rich variety and precious care that we give to the interior of our houses, the exterior of our homes is often forgotten? When we began researching a TV programme looking at the front of people's houses, we found endless semi-detached homes blending into a monotony of faceless buildings. Areas were suffering from a lack of identity or sense of place. Why was there no personalization of the houses themselves?

Front of House set out to challenge people's perceptions and ideas about what could be done to the exterior of a building. The programme asked 20 homeowners to have the fronts of their houses and front gardens redesigned based on an account of who they were, their likes, hobbies and interests. Oliver and Lisa then used this information to redesign the appearance of the houses to reflect the personalities and tastes of the owners: 'We wanted to test the notions of convention and promote self-expression. The streets of the UK are so often a uniform experience. Self-expression is kept to the interior of a building and the exterior is often an area of neglect where self-expression is kept to a minimum.'

Front of House aimed to encourage people to be creative and to express themselves through the fabric of their house. This book provides further ideas, help and advice for anyone inspired to carry out their own works. We use case studies to describe many of the different situations encountered during the programme, giving background details to the process and the thinking behind the different designs.

By personalising our homes, we can represent the vast diversity of tastes, ages and cultures that make up the unique character of British towns today. Your home is your chance to express yourself and to contribute to the exciting cultural mix.

We all have a responsibility to our direct and wider environment. The range of housing available in Britain rarely reflects our individuality – thousands of homes on hundreds of streets all look the same. There's little individuality, self-expression and, very often, very little pride taken in the front of our houses. Even small changes can make a real difference. We all make individual creative decisions every day from what we wear, to what we eat, and it's just as easy to make decisions about the way our homes look, so let's start to make a creative contribution to our surroundings.

WHY CHANGE THE FRONT OF YOUR HOUSE?

The front of your house is a connection with your street – it is the face that you present to others. It can express your character, tastes, interests, wealth, fears and even aspirations. Some people prefer to present an impersonal, characterless, façade, but others may be more flamboyant and may want their house to represent an element of their character – be it friendly, welcoming, artistic, romantic or traditional.

In some areas a whole street may already have been appropriated by a particular design aesthetic, such as in Notting Hill, London, where the houses have been painted in different shades. The overall look is quirky and creates a stunning effect that shows an idea of community and togetherness. This can make an area highly sought-after.

Adding your own expression brings another layer to the history of your home. It is important that you gain an understanding of your house's historical context so you can work within the original design parameters and style, otherwise it can look unbalanced. Most houses are already a mixture of styles adopted from the past, so when you add your own touch you are leaving a mark of time and telling a story for future generations.

NEIGHBOURHOODS, SUBURBS AND CITIES

British cities started to lose popularity at the turn of the 19th century. Inner city slums were full of disease, 'questionable behaviour' and an increasing population. The countryside took on a new appeal as space for recreation and leisure.

Ownership of early suburban houses was seen as a status symbol and so the developer of the 1840s used a great deal of ornamentation on the façades to appeal to the growing wealthy class. As the social climate changed, families no longer had live-in servants and houses became smaller for the fewer people living in them.

A few philanthropic individuals created utopian ideals: countryside homes for people to live in that were actually within the city or on its outskirts. These were known as 'garden suburbs' and included places such as Hampstead Garden Suburb and Letchworth. The designs of the houses took inspiration from traditional countryside dwellings to recreate the idyllic country retreat, but within the city.

These provided the models of the suburbs that we see today, where individual houses have protected garden spaces and the streets have trees and sometimes communal grassed areas.

Far left: Bonnington Square is a unique place in London where the residents have populated the pavements with areas of exotic planting, seating and artwork.

Left: Hampstead Garden suburb is an example of a utopian ideal to create desirable country-style suburbs close to city centres.

IDENTIFYING THE STYLE OF YOUR HOUSE

Not all houses are works of art, but they do all have an intrinsic character of their own – either because of the building technique employed or because of some architectural effect or functionality.

Left: A Georgian terrace house consists of a simple elegant flat façade with a regularity in the heights of windows and floor levels.

Right: A typical Victorian terrace sought to break up the flatness of the façade by introducing bay windows.

The face of your house reflects the climate, geology, craftsmanship, materials, fashions and laws that were current when it was built. To destroy or change this is to lose or alter evidence of the past. That's not to say we should live in museums, but before beginning a radical overhaul it is worth knowing what you are starting with. Changes in design can usually be traced back to social change, economic climate and industrial progress; one or more of which would have influenced the designers, artists and developers of the time.

THE GEORGIAN ERA

During this period, the designs for the façade and the plan of the house were two separate concerns. The overall composition of the front was the most important concern and reflected current interest in the classic traditions of Greek and Roman architecture with its emphasis on composition and order. Elements of decoration were in the detail: the cornices, door and window surrounds, the choice of material and the colour. The façade had little to do with the people living inside except to indicate their status. Groups of houses often shared a façade to look as if it were really one large house. These terraces often used very few contrasting materials, and although the effect was simple and grand, it tended towards uniformity.

In late Georgian and Regency terraces, the landscape garden had a big influence, so both the house and its setting were given equal importance. Circuses and squares became popular, taking full advantage of their site. Regency houses introduced balconies and wrought ironwork, often inspired by individuals who had travelled abroad and seen different styles. Many of these types of houses can still be seen in London, and in spa towns such as Bath and Brighton.

THE VICTORIAN ERA

Due to a massive building boom at the time, Victorian housing is by far the most common in Britain. The style grew out of revivals of the past, and designs took reference from the ornate and expressive Renaissance period and austere Gothic architecture. Victorian housing incorporates two different elements: the country house, which is individually styled, and the flat-fronted terraces, which were built for lower social classes. An increase in general mobility and ease of transport meant that houses were no longer built of local building materials, but of materials such as brick.

THE EDWARDIAN ERA

In the 19th century a growing number of single suburban houses were built that were based on the rambling designs of buildings in the countryside. This development was influenced by the Arts and Crafts movement, which encouraged a style that reflected the individual. A more romantic rural style influenced both house design and the materials used. Even though they were in semi-urban locations, these homes felt more rural in spirit.

THE MODERN MOVEMENT (ART DECO)

After World War I, values, influence and taste were reassessed. Ornamentation was associated with false wealth and social hierarchy, so a new style evolved. Emphasis was given to funtion and form, which is why many façades seem expressionless. A functional approach was taken to move alongside the fast progression of technology; houses were seen as vehicles for living and interiors often received more thought than façades. Modern materials and methods such as concrete and prefabrication were experimented with, to allow houses to be cheaper and more efficient. Modernist houses were generally very rectilinear constructions, with strong horizontal lines, flat roofs, and simple façades.

JACOBETHAN STYLE

Home ownership made a vast difference to attitudes and market forces in style and design of the home. The individual market demanded the ideal of a picturesque image of a country cottage – something cosy and intimate. The styles therefore reflected the rural aesthetic and copied the vernacular architecture of the country that looked back to the Jacobean and Tudor eras. Developers and designers revisited traditional building types for inspiration, combining the feel of a historic exterior with a modern interior.

Many buildings were made of red brick, with long, tiled, sloping roofs, and semi-timbered façades and porches.

CURRENT STYLES

Today, house styles are eclectic. Developers frequently concentrate on reproducing pastiches of classical style which is popular because of the comfort of the familiar and the perceived value. Architects are exploring new technologies and materials to find new expressions for housing. Examples include Bed-zed, an environmental housing project where the majority of the power is generated on the site and the buildings are constructed from environmental materials.

Far left: A Jacobethan house has a rustic aesthetic of red brick and a semi-timbered projecting bay. The exposed black timbers are just ornamentation but are reminiscent of the exposed timbers of Tudor houses.

Left: Greenwich Millennium Village is a colourful, diverse, modern neighbourhood that is both environmentally friendly and distinctive.

A QUICK GUIDE TO BUILDING STYLES

Tudor and Jacobean (1495–1625): Houses were mainly timber-framed, using wattle and daub technique.

Baroque (1625–1714): External ornamentation was used to complement internal design – for example, the proportion and grandeur of a window tended to reflect the importance of the room within. Many houses were rebuilt using stone or brick.

Georgian (1714–1811): Georgian houses typically had a plain façade and were designed symmetrically, with regular, carefully proportioned windows and delicate detailing. Front doors were plain.

Regency (1811–1837): French architecture, decoration and a taste for the exotic were all popular at this time. Rich decoration was often contrasted with plain areas of brick or fashionable stucco.

Victorian (1837–1901): The Victorians looked to break up the flatness of the façade with the introduction of bay or oriel windows, which projected into the street. Porches were recessed into the façade and there was frequently ornamentation in plasterwork around the doors and windows. This was also the era of pointed and curved arches.

Arts and Crafts (1860–1925): The Arts and Crafts movement championed fine craftsmanship and the use of fine and attractive building materials.

Art Nouveau (1888–1905): This style is characterized by exuberant, curvilinear forms based on organic lines. In Britain, Art Nouveau style was often used only on details and was more popular as an overall style on the Continent.

Edwardian (1901–1914): Late-Edwardian is defined by red brick buildings with white stone dressings.

Art Deco (1920–1935): This style was named after the Paris exhibition of decorative and industrial styles and was epitomised by suntrap strip steel framed windows (many of which curved), flat roofs and decorative touches such as sunray patterns. Many designs were inspired by the streamline forms found in the new technology of the time, such as aeroplanes, cars and cruise ships.

The Modern Movement (1920–1965): This style was a self-conscious move away from the past. Designers felt a need to express the essence of the machine age. The new architecture relied on space, proportion, composition and smooth surfaces.

Post-Modern (1950–1990): Designers tired of the restrictions of modernism sought to generate a new 'anything goes' aesthetic. Styles include ironic refernces to past design features and often the simplification of classic elements.

CASE STUDY
Identifying Your House

Kay's suburban house has a strong design, which clearly dates from the Art Deco period of the 1920s and 30s. The lines and curves of the building, with striped horizontal bands, reflect the mood and aesthetic of this period and the metal-framed suntrap windows are a typical feature. Many buildings during this period took their design inspiration from boats, trains and other vehicles. The Art Deco period was a time of change in the automotive industry and the world seemed to be speeding up. This was reflected in design through the use of curves and aerodynamic styling.

If you are working within a strong historic tradition, then knowing a little about it can provide guidance for your design. However, it can also make it harder as you'll need to be sensitive to the original design and era of your home.

Kay's house was designed with this in mind and the chosen colours and stencil patterns that were used on the house all reference the Art Deco period to create a harmonious overall look.

Oliver was also keen to add a design touch that related to an aspect of Kay's personality as a passionate salsa dancer. He used a resin-bonded glass chip material in a shade of blue that would match the house to produce a series of inset dance steps on the driveway (see also 'Driveways', pages 123–125). Now, every time Kay leaves or returns home she will be reminded of what it is that really makes her feel alive, and guests will know of her dancing passion. This contemporary detail subtly complimented the period architecture and expressed the character of the house owner.

IMPACT ON THE NEIGHBOURHOOD

Before beginning to design, there are a number of things to consider. One of the most important is the wider context of your changes – how will they affect the local environment?

The combined and harmonious design of these two houses gives a sense of unity and community to the neighbourhood.

A house in a country landscape is often set on its own and has a relationship and dynamic with the scenery around it. However, a house in a town, city or village is is not an individual unit but one of many. When you look down a street the houses often take a similar form and it is often difficult to distinguish one from the next. The heights are roughly the same, the line of the street is maintained and the front gardens will be of a similar size. However, on closer inspection the details often vary from one house to another. The front doors are all different, the porches have been individualized and some people prefer a hard landscape for their garden to one with planted shrubs and flowers. These details provide visual interest and character to the street.

It is worth remembering that on a wider scale the image of the street will not change regardless of how you choose to treat an individual façade and front garden. The overall effect will still be one of unity because even if houses have been built at different times, renovated or added to, the new and old will have a relationship to one another through their overall proportions or original style.

However, redesigning the exterior of your building can have a huge impact on your immediate neighbours. There can be a knock-on effect – if one person does something then others may follow. Small adjustments can kick-start the regeneration of an entire street or neighbourhood.

If you live in a terrace or semi-detached house discuss your ideas with your neighbours; they may also want to do work to their house. Joining together may not only reduce the cost of works, but will also have a positive effect on your property if others around it also look their best. Julia and Bernadette's houses (above) were semi-detached and work was carried out across both properties to create the appearance of one much larger house. In addition, a veranda and pergola were constructed, stretching across both houses so that both families could use the area as a social space.

Finally, it is certainly worth remembering that people are different and that each person has the right to individuality and self-expression, even if you do not like what they create. It is helpful to be tolerant and discuss options if one party is unhappy. See if you can work out a compromise that still allows creative flair without causing conflict between you and your neighbours.

Some people think that their way of seeing things is the only way, and therefore do not appreciate people expressing their individuality. Likewise, it is easy to believe that we have the right to do what we like without taking into consideration the consequences on the wider community. This is a difficult balance to get right but the issue is well worth bearing in mind when doing up our own houses.

QUALITY OF OUR ENVIRONMENT

Your quality of environment is largely determined by the treatment of the front of your house and garden. The boundary wall can be designed to create a safe boundary that protects the property without blocking all views to the street. Likewise, the treatment of your front door is the first point of contact visitors have when arriving at your home. We all want our windows to provide us with the ability to see out, as well as to allow the maximum amount of light to flood in.

The way you choose to define the boundaries of your property will in turn determine the perception of your street and neighbourhood. A house surrounded by high walls, gates and tall hedges creates an atmosphere of uneasiness both for passers-by and for the inhabitants. The message given out by the homeowner is that they have something to hide, and that the area is one where crime is rife.

In Europe, the space in front of the house is used much more than in Britain. For example, in Italy it is common to see people sitting outside the front of their houses, watching the world go by, whilst in the Netherlands many housing projects encourage the use of the front of the house by designing planters, safe storage and seating in the front gardens.

HOW DOES THIS AFFECT THE VALUE OF YOUR HOME?

Houses were often valued for their functional benefits and their location but not necessarily for their design. This is changing as we become more design-conscious both of interiors and, now, exteriors.

Different styles of housing are often associated with hierarchy, wealth and status. For many years, buildings were designed to reflect the wealth and status of the homeowner, and this attitude is deeply rooted in our society. For example, when stone was too expensive to build with, a render with grooves in it, made to look like stone (known as stucco), was applied in order to give an impression of wealth.

Nowadays it is common to see classical columns added to the front of a new porch in order to add grandeur to the entrance. Sometimes this has the desired effect, but often the classical addition does not fit comfortably with the original design of the house. Similarly, estate agents are finding that UPVC windows have reduced the value of many properties because of their appearance and the lack of sympathy with the original character of the house.

The quality of the appearance of the house will affect the value of your home. With so many similar properties on the market, adding an element of design can make your house stand out. One-off houses designed by individual architects attract a premium because the designers have thought about the quality of the space both internally and externally.

CULTURAL CONTEXT

The design of houses around the world reflects a variety of traditions, religions, climates and uses. Houses are attributed with different meanings and symbols. The door is especially important, as it is the threshold between inside and out: public and private worlds. Many rituals occur at this threshold, including taking off shoes, welcoming the occupants and an acknowledgment of entering the sanctity and privacy of a home.

In countries such as India and Nepal, the outside of the house is seen as sacred; colourful shrines are often built at the entrance to protect the house and its occupants. There is a Jewish tradition of placing a 'mezuzah' – a prayer – inside a small rectangular box on the door frame of the front door as a constant reminder of the presence of God.

Sometimes we choose to decorate the fronts of our houses because of a festival or tradition. At Christmas time, lights go up and Christmas trees are placed in the front garden or front windows, brightening up the dark, cold winter nights. Similarly at the Hindu festival of Diwali – the festival of light – doorways are decorated with colourful patterns (*Rangoli*) to welcome *Lakshemi*, the goddess of wealth and prosperity.

Whilst it can be easy to go over the top with the decorations – as is frequently seen at Christmas with extravagant displays of light that use thousands of watts of energy, decorating the front of your house can be a real sign of an active and desirable neighbourhood – a neighbourhood that is keen to show a public presence and to

The decorative Christmas wreath, fairy lights and trees give this door a real sense of festive welcome.

participate in social customs and that shows a sense of solidarity and community. It can put out a strong and positive message to all who enter the area that the inhabitants are attentive and care about the community and environment, making it feel both friendlier and safer. There are a variety of festivals that communities can participate in across the year, from Christmas to Easter to Halloween – it will bring your home and the whole neighbourhood alive.

You could even organize a summer or festive street party and decorate your street accordingly. It'll be a great chance to meet the neighbourhood and rouse some community spirit – who knows what sort of positive aspects may come from it?

UNLEASHING YOUR CREATIVE POTENTIAL

This eccentric design created a talking point in the city of Oxford, but may not be quite to everyones liking!

We all have creative potential, whether it's expressed in writing, drawing or conversation, but we often overlook what makes us unique.

We all wear different clothes, have different hairstyles and spend our free time differently. Yet we often choose to keep ourselves very private. When someone decides to make a bold personal statement on the front of their house it becomes a shared public experience. People usually find it easier to reflect their tastes in design through the interior decoration of their homes. However, there are many ways of expressing your personality on the front of your house, from the smallest detail like changing the design of the house number, to the boldest statement covering the entire façade. Anyone can think about design, so get inspired by jotting ideas down on paper and consulting books and magazines. There are also many people whose professional advice you can seek before undertaking any major change.

Think about what you want to say – express your character and try to create an equal interest between inside and outside. Being noticed is not necessarily a bad thing, particularly if people think the front of your house improves the quality of the neighbourhood!

WHAT TYPE OF STYLE INTERESTS YOU?

Look around you at different styles and designs of house. It is often possible to apply your own style to your house. Defining your tastes and sense of style is a good start to a design.

What sort of design style do you feel comfortable with; what gets you really excited?

There are a variety of different styles that you could choose from for the front of your house. Some of these may be similar to those that you've applied on the interior – this could prove to be key when deciding how to approach the exterior.

Once you know the style you are interested in, do some research and consider exactly what it is that makes up that particular look. Ask yourself the following questions:

- What colour should the walls be?
- What type of cladding would I like to add?
- Does the design need additional decorative details?
- What should the doorway look like?
- What type of plants and hard landscaping would be appropriate?

Try piecing together a concept board (much in the same way that you might for an interior design makeover), that incorporates colours, materials, any furniture, plants, and anything else that catches your eye and that you feel would be appropriate to the style of your design. Use images from magazines, or from pictures that you have taken.

Key interior styles are contemporary, natural, shabby chic, rustic, romantic, minimalist, urban or even that of the global traveller, complete with wood carvings from the other side of the world. Ultimately, go with whatever you feel most comfortable with, and what seems most appropriate for the front of your house.

CASE STUDY
A house for Goths

Ange and Lee are Goths and wanted to have
their house redesigned so that their style could
be reflected on the outside of the property.
Ange is a practising ghost hunter with a passion
for the supernatural, whilst Lee collects all types
of horror movies and loves thrash metal music.
Their interest in the Gothic style, however, was
far from reflected in their home. The new design
took original black-and-white horror B-movies
as a source point. All the colour of the house
has been de-saturated and the house painted
in tones of a ghostly grey. The tongue-in-cheek
design references various movies in subtle and
fun ways to give an overall impression of a haunted
house. Net curtains were chosen as window
coverings – the nets were given a very light
grey colour to blend in with the overall effect.
Net curtains have an old-fashioned look that
suit this design perfectly, whilst also conjuring
images of Alfred Hitchcock's film *Psycho*.

In addition to this the house was adorned
with ornate classical style mirrors (painted a
ghostly grey, of course!) that were suspended
from the facade at a high level to reflect the
sky – conjuring up a sense of spooky emptiness.

A sense of fun was also added through the
use of some fake crows, which were attached
to the doorway and a single line of blood-red
paint that appeared to trickle from the first floor
window. The garden was enclosed by a Victorian
cast iron style fence and contained a fire pit,
some wonderfully crafted stocks to sit on and
a dark pond that was underlit, casting a ghostly
light though the smoke produced by a machine
located just beneath the waterline.

As Ange and Lee were initially keen for their
house to reflect the feel of a haunted house with
a graveyard for a garden, Lisa and Oliver worked
hard to find an acceptable design solution that
felt spooky whilst not being outright scary, and
allowing Ange and Lee to express themselves on
the façade and garden of their home to all those
who dared to enter!

CASE STUDY
An eccentric house

Eccentricity is often a trait that manifests itself visibly and makes someone stand out from the crowd. This may be because of the way a person dresses, their interests, their occupation, their mannerisms or perhaps how their home looks. Quirky eccentricity is a British trait that adds colour to our lives. After all, do we really all want to be the same?

Chris's house presented us with an opportunity to work with the eccentricity of the client. Chris is a flamboyant man who loves off-road driving, old-style slapstick comedy, travel, golf and who is a DJ in his spare time. His sense of fun required an equally fun design. His house presented a blank canvas as it was not of any particular period and did not require any elements to be preserved.

The design is an ironic conglomeration of elements of different periods. A classical portico added to the front of the house immediately makes a dramatic statement. By painting it dark blue and giving a background of painted stripes on the façade of the building, the effect of adding the portico becomes ironic. The scale of the portico is disproportionate to the rest of the house, adding to the sense of curiousness of the house as a whole. Touches such as the antlers over the front door and painted corbels beneath the windows also reference English country manor-style in a humorous way.

THINK SMALL – LET THE IDEA GROW

If re-designing the front of your home presents you with an enormous challenge that appears insurmountable, start by thinking small and allowing the ideas to grow. Focus on details such as the front door or house number. Eve Rowe was a motorbike fan – by adding bike mirrors and headlamps around the door a distinct feature was created that expressed her tastes (see page 106).

You may want to take inspiration from your interior too and co-ordinate the inside with the exterior to show that you have thought the design through carefully.

FINAL NOTE

Most houses are a conglomeration of styles. For example, a house may have taken influences from the Georgian period (classical porch), included some Victorian (bay window) and combined this with a timber-slatted country cottage-style front door. Although these styles do not belong within the same time-frame, developers may have used them together in order to fulfil all the expectations of would-be buyers. Developers interpret designs to give people what they think they want, so you should not be too precious about adding your own interpretation, which is just as valid. You need to find a balance between adding your own creative input that gives the house an element of individuality whilst maintaining the harmony of the street.

What we see today, unlike in any previous era, is the availability of a huge variety of materials, building techniques and technology. In the past, houses often reflected the stage of technological improvement; for example, when sash windows were invented, they appeared in all houses. Nowadays we have new materials, but our houses still reflect the styles of the past hundred or more years.

SUMMARY: MAKING DECISIONS

- Consider the necessary lifespan of the proposed works.
- Are you going to restore and renovate, and if so, how long do you wish any changes you make to last?
- How long are you planning to stay in your house? If it is your permanent home perhaps a really unique idea will suit you, but if you are thinking of selling then consider your potential market.
- Think about your neighbourhood and how the design will affect both you and the surrounding area.
- Think about your tastes, style and character and choose the materials to express this.
- Muted natural tonal colour schemes will be more acceptable to people in general, whilst brighter more vivid or contrasting colours will liven up the neighbourhood.
- Take a fresh look at your house and be critical. Consider how you could make it more welcoming for you and your guests.
- Make a special effort to consider the design of the front entrance area, as this is where the first impressions will be solidified.

CHAPTER 2
GETTING
STARTED

The key to a successful design project is preparation. A professional designer will always arrive on a site with a clear plan as to how to carry out the intended design, to a high quality, in the time available and to budget. The more decisions you make prior to starting the job, the easier it will be.

Although some of the points made here may seem scary, don't be put off, as redesigning or making over the front of your house is highly achievable and incredibly satisfying, once completed.

PLANNING THE JOB

Doing up the front of your house differs in a few ways from carrying out an interior design project, so you need to consider these before starting work.

You may need to contact your local authority, as dealing with an exterior will have an impact on the general environment of the street, and the general safety of the work will need to be considered. You will have to make sure that your materials are able to stand up to the elements long-term and, ideally, you should try to carry out the work in the drier months of the year.

Before starting any work you must be sure you have a definite plan. Know your budget and be clear about your intentions. It is important that you follow these in order for the design to be completed successfully. Having said this, things don't always turn out as planned so you will have to be flexible. Dealing with properties of any age invariably brings up unforeseen problems, so factor in a contingency of time and money to cover these. Think carefully about what you want to achieve. It may be that due to disrepair a change is necessary, or you may need to add a porch for storage, or you might just want to brighten up the wall colour. Once your wish list has been written you can then begin to develop your ideas. Do some research into the historic origins of your house and any regulations that need to be complied with. Then source the best contractor for the job. You are now ready to begin.

FINDING OUT ABOUT THE HISTORY OF YOUR HOUSE

A good place to start researching the history of your house is the local public library. There is normally a historical section with building records where you can find your property's date of construction and the name of its architect and builder. Your local planning authority may also be helpful. It can advise on the architectural merits of particular buildings in the area and it keeps details of any changes that have been made to the dwelling if planning permission was applied for. If the house was built recently they will have copies of the drawings. The Building Control department may also have copies of drawings and information on your house, especially if works have been carried out to the house or if it is newly built.

You could also ask neighbours for possible information about your property. Have a look at their houses for indications of surviving original features which may be lacking from your own home.

Your local library might have archival photos of the area which would be one way to gain an impression of the original appearance of your house or neighbourhood.

STEPS TO TAKE WHEN THINKING ABOUT YOUR FRONT OF HOUSE

1 Study the design of your house to see what improvements need to be made. Does an unsightly porch need to be removed, cables tidied up or a television aerial placed in a better position? Is the paint peeling or looking tired? Is there damp or cracking? (See Structural and Surface Defects, pages 34–5.) Some internal defects will be affected by the external state of your home, so make a clear list of any issues.

2 What functional aspects do you require? Bike or bin storage, a new front gate, off-street parking or better lighting? Spend time considering what needs to be incorporated.

3 It may now be worth writing out your wish list. Would you like to change the front door, paint the windows or add expression and colour to the front façade or the front garden? Consider how you could make your house more beautiful.

4 Find a balance between your budget and timescale. You could consider getting in contractors to complete all the work in one go, which could be cheaper in the long run, or perhaps some aspects need urgent attention while others can take place later when you have saved some more money. It may be possible to undertake a few things on the wish list as well as sort out the problem matters.

5 Find out about the history of your house. This can help you understand its original design aesthetic including the style of the front door and even its colour. It may be that over the years the original interesting brickwork has been covered up with a rendered exterior. This knowledge can help you to plan where you want to take the house in the future – what you wish to conserve, reinstate or change.

6 Before beginning it is worth checking with your local planning office whether your house is scheduled as a building of architectural interest. Alternatively, the area in which your house is situated may have been given a conservation listing. If this is the case there will be a different set of rules to guide your design. Speak to the planning officer for detailed advice and information. It may also be possible to get a grant towards the work from your local council's conservation department if the works are reinstating the original character of the house.

7 If you would rather seek professional advice on improving the visual appearance of your house, choose an architect or designer who has a sense of history and good eye for colour and graphics. A professional can produce a set of drawings that can show you what the house will look like with the alterations. Alternatively, they can advise about replacing elements of your house in order to regain its original historic appearance. A landscape architect or gardener can help to design the hard and soft surfaces of the garden.

You are now ready to begin to design.

LEGISLATION – DOS AND DON'TS

Not all work requires official permission but it is always worth checking with the relevant local authority whether permissions might apply to your proposed works. Be careful, because if you build something without obtaining permission first you may be forced to put things right later or even to remove the building or structure altogether.

Planning permission

Planning departments and laws are set up to protect the appearance, quality and design of the general environment (in this case, your street), while still allowing individuals a reasonable degree of freedom to alter their property. Legislation was set up from the 19th century to take a holistic view of development, maintain a sense of order in our cities, protect the countryside and regulate excessive development.

Protected areas

Check whether your house falls within a specially protected area where extra planning restrictions apply. These include Conservation Areas, National Parks and Areas of Outstanding Beauty. There are also different requirements if your house is a listed building. In order to be listed a building must be of architectural or historical importance. It could be listed because it has some stylistic value or for social reasons (such as what the building stood for in society, its historical significance or who designed it). The building could also be listed because it was technically innovative. There are three types of listing depending on the importance of the property: Grade I, Grade II and Grade II*. Each of these needs to be treated differently, so talk to your planning department for more information.

Often alterations within these areas will need to be considered on their visual grounds in relation to the original property and may include the landscape around the house and the front walls.

Minor changes

When you have established you are not in one of these areas, certain types of change are permitted without planning permission. These are known as Permitted Development Rights and cover:

- Most repairs and maintenance
- Minor improvements such as painting your house or replacing windows
- Porches of a certain size
- Hard and soft landscaping (unless it changes the use of the land in some way, such as in the case of business parking)
- Some garages within the limits of the requirements
- Temporary structures. This applies to houses and not flats or maisonettes. In general you need permission to build closer to the street than the line of your house with any permanent structure unless this is a porch or temporary structure.

A porch needs planning permission if it has a ground area greater than 3sq m (32.3sq ft), or is higher than 2m (6.6ft) or if it would be closer than 2m (6.6ft) from the boundary to the street. A boundary fence, wall or gate needs permission if it is over 1m (3.3ft) high next to the street or 2m (6.6ft) high elsewhere. There are no permissions needed for planting.

The exception to all these rules is if your house has any special protections.

Contact the planning department for information on how to make an application. You should get a response in around eight weeks. An easy-to-read brochure is available from most planning offices if you need further detailed information. The general rule is that if you have any doubts, or are considering any work on the front of your house, it is better to contact your planning authority to discuss the plans informally. It shouldn't cost you anything, and will put your mind at rest – better safe than sorry!

Building Control permissions

Building Regulations relate to how a building stays up, its efficiency and its safety. They include areas such as the structure of any new buildings, means of escape and the fire integrity of the building (ventilation and heat loss, glazing and disabled access). In addition you need approval if you are covering over any sewer or drain. For any new construction works, contact your local Building Control department to discuss whether you need approvals – again, you may find an informal meeting helpful to clarify your position. Complicated works require drawings to be submitted but otherwise an officer will come and inspect any relevant works. An explanatory booklet is available from the Planning and Building Control departments. Building Regulations application forms can also be obtained from your local planning office.

It is essential that any work meets the Building Regulations requirements so that you can obtain a certificate that confirms that the work was carried out to the approved standards. This is necessary both for insurance purposes, and when you come to sell your home.

Party Wall agreement

This is required when the work you are planning affects a wall that you share with a neighbour – a wall that sits on the boundary line between two adjacent properties. There is either a 'party wall' – a wall that you can build off – or a 'party fence wall' – one that you don't support from, like a garden wall. When you decide to do works to this wall you must inform your neighbour. If they do not agree, a Party Wall agreement can be drawn up to protect both parties. To obtain such an agreement you will need to instruct a surveyor (at your cost) to inspect both your property and that of your neighbour. A letter is then signed by each party. If your neighbour verbally agrees to the work then make sure you get him or her to sign some drawings or a letter of intent otherwise the agreement may not be valid.

If you are only altering your fences, look at your property deeds to see which fence is your responsibility, although, for the sake of neighbourly relations, you should check with your neighbours and inform them of any work you might be doing.

Right to light

Right to light entitles an owner to prevent his or her neighbour from building anything that will obstruct the flow of light through particular windows. The nature and use of a building will determine the amount of light entitlement, but this is usually considered to be a level sufficient for comfortable use and enjoyment. It is measured as the light flow into the window without interruption at an angle of 45 degrees from the horizontal, and is measured at the sill. This is unlikely to affect you unless you are building something substantial on to the front of the house, such as a garage.

CASE STUDY
Planning a nautical house

The owner of this house was a boat builder, which offered an opportunity to give his house a clear identity. The extension appeared to be a later addition to the house, and the garage doors and paintwork were in need of maintenance. It was therefore decided to highlight the extension as a separate part of the house, but connect it to elements of the entrance and garden.

For all the houses on *Front of House* the planning authorities were consulted early on. Local authority rules differ across the country and it is important to discuss your plans. This house was not in a conservation area so the colour scheme was not a concern but the additional cladding proposed for the extension was, as the planners were worried that this would extend the line of the property out towards the street. However, as the original porch of this house projected out beyond the line of the extension, seen at the junction between the two, the planners permitted the cladding to extend

out to the 'line of the front of the house' without us having to apply for planning permission.

Ship-lap timber was clad horizontally over the entire extension to give a uniform appearance to the entire façade, including the garage doors. Marine fittings, such as the portholes and lights, added a sense of fun. The colours of the timber and front door were chosen to complement the original brickwork of the porch and the bright yellow front door provided a positive and welcoming entrance. The nautical theme carried on into the garden, with planting that you might find near a beach and the same timber clad the front wall. As a final touch the door number was added by branding it into the timber cladding on the garage doors. A local blacksmith helped out by providing the number in steel.

The result was a contemporary house that combined the character of the owner with the aesthetic needs of the property, and provided a cheerful bright addition to the street.

THE DESIGN PROCESS

A blank sheet of paper can be a rather daunting start to any design.

If you are to undertake a redesign of part of or the entire front of your house and garden then you will need to become familiar with techniques that allow you to experiment with and envisage the design options. A sketch will help you to visualize the final product, test ideas and experiment before committing to one design. It can also be useful to discuss your ideas with a builder or gardener.

Before making a start it is important to look closely at your own house as viewed from the street. Next examine its relationship with its neighbours and finally with the whole street. We recommend that you take photos from a number of angles and various distances to get an all-round overall picture.

The next stage is to try sketching out your ideas. This can be done in a number of ways. Try making a photocopy enlargement of the best view of the whole house showing the properties next to it. Take a few copies of this image so that you can really experiment by drawing directly on to them. Apply different colours and trace different forms, shapes, images and materials. Alternatively, you can buy some tracing paper or layout paper and draw the outline of the house (preferably from the enlarged photocopy) and work on that. If you have computer skills then a good way to visualize ideas is by scanning in the photo and then working on it using Photoshop, or other imaging programmes.

Sources of inspiration

There are a number of ways you can go about finding inspiration.
- Keep a scrapbook of pictures of designs, materials and products you may have seen. Take ideas from magazines, or your own photos. You may wish to create a mood board to focus the ideas on to one area.
- Get together with friends and brainstorm – it is amazing how productive this can be, and it will help you to consider your ideas clearly and with an open mind.
- Think about your own interests and hobbies and see if they can be reflected in the design.
- Have a look at the case studies in this book.
- Go to shops that sell appropriate materials and browse the products and fittings. Think laterally and see if you can use the materials in a different way from that which they were intended for.
- Look at design books and magazines for ideas – you can take elements from different designs and put them together to create your own.

We would recommend concentrating on a single idea in order to have a strong concept that holds together; often, too many ideas can be very confusing and lead to a less than harmonious finished design.

See how your design relates to your neighbours' properties and the original features of your own house. This is especially important if you live in a semi-detached house. It is always a good idea to ask the opinion of the neighbours and some trusted friends, especially those with design experience.

CASE STUDY
Giving your house a Beachcomber theme

Giving the design of your house a theme can add a quirky element to a street and create a sense of fun and frivolity. However, themes are often highly personalized so do not suit all tastes, so if you are trying to sell your house, be careful.

Nikki and Colin's house is situated not far from the sea near Norwich in Norfolk. They are lovers of nature and travel, so the house was given a tactile and coastal appearance using the idea of a secluded, weathered beach house and including sea-themed features. The colour scheme and chosen materials are very natural, suggesting sand dunes, pebbles, driftwood, grasses growing amongst the dunes and shadows of seagulls flying overhead. The pebble tiling around both doorways placed particular emphasis on framing the front door and the

window coverings were changed to fit with the overall design of the house: in this case woven split bamboo blinds were fitted that also matched the soft, shabby chic interior.

The design of the garden related to that of the house by using railway sleepers inset into the drive infilled with loose shingle, steel mesh gabions filled with soft rounded pebbles, and slate flower beds (see also page 118). Additional pieces were added that complemented the house, including rusty chains, eight foot lengths of drift wood standing vertical, rusted anchors and curios of rusted steel. The edge of the street was defined with a wavey-edged timber fence, which echoed the movement of the sea.

The overall effect was an asymmetric design which joined the extension on the right with the rest of the house.

HOW TO DECIDE WHAT COLOUR TO USE

Colour is one of the key ways to make a dramatic and cost-effective change to the front of your house. It can tie it in with neighbouring houses, make it stand out, display a house number or painted graphic, or communicate your passions and interests. Remember that, unlike a room, your house is not seen in isolation – the colour of the roof, the ground and the sky will all interact with the colour you choose to paint your house. In addition, the kind of daylight we experience in the UK may affect the way the colour looks.

The addition of the red porch on Jason and Kate's house added vibrancy and individuality without overwhelming the street.

Responding to colour

The colour you see depends on a number of factors: the light quality, your eyesight and ability to distinguish colour differences, your emotional response and also your memory of association with particular colours. The emotional responses might be as simple as blues signifying cool and expansiveness because of their association with water and sky, and reds equating with warmth.

In general, muted coloured houses tend to be more popular (this can be important if you wish to get on with your neighbour!), as are colours inspired by nature. A darker background colour accented by a bright colour will add life, vibrancy and personality.

COLOUR TIPS

- Light colours can make your house seem larger. Darker shades are best for accenting recesses, while lighter tones will highlight details that project from the wall surface.
- Contrasting or complementary colours will draw attention to architectural details; they might be a little unsettling but they are very lively. Examples can be seen throughout history such as the traditional black and white house decoration in Cumbria, and green woodwork on a red brick house.
- If you want to stay safe, consider working with a single colour family and using a tonal colour scheme that will be easy on the eye.

- For some accents, try using a darker or lighter shade instead of a different colour. Small areas of white will always provide a sparkle when used in conjunction with a darker colour.
- The more intense a colour, the more likely it is to fade. After a few years, vivid blues and deep reds will seem more subdued when they were first painted.
- Colour swatches look very different when they are brought out of the shop and viewed in natural sunlight. Colours appear lighter on large surfaces than they do on small samples. It is best to test your selected colour in one area before buying the paint.

DRAWINGS TO SCALE

Not all design changes need to have scale drawings, especially if you are only making minor alterations. However, if you have more ambitious plans then these drawings will certainly be a useful way to communicate your ideas.

A drawing to scale is useful in two main ways. Firstly it briefs a builder to construct your design and secondly it will help you to calculate the quantities and costs of the materials you require.

There are two types of drawing that you may need:
A plan. A measured map or layout of the ground surface, drawn as if you are looking straight down from above on to the house and garden. This will show the layout of the front garden design, any paths, the boundary edge of your property and the edge of your house.
An elevation. A measured drawing of the front face (façade) of your house where any projecting bays or areas are seen as flat surfaces not in perspective.

To find the height of your house, take a photo of someone standing in front of it with a tape measure to show the scale. You can then apply a grid to the picture to find out the total height.

To obtain the information for these drawings you will have to measure the front of your house and the front garden. Draw a sketch and mark on the dimensions. Then make your scale drawing. This is an exact representation of the house but scaled down to fit on to a sheet of paper. The easiest way is to use squared paper and use a scale where every four squares on the paper represent one metre of your house, then transfer all the measurements from your initial sketch on to the drawing.

Then overlay this with tracing paper and experiment with designs, showing both features that are staying and those that are changing.

If you label the drawing with all the materials and dimensions, a builder can look to see what your intentions are. You can also measure the areas for each material to assist in costing the job.

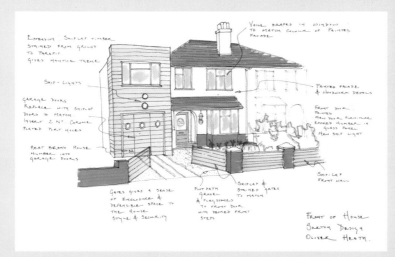

An initial design sketch is a great way to represent and test out the impact that different materials and colours will have on the front of your house. It will clearly show the visual appearance of the proposed design which will be a great help when you are trying to communicate your ideas to your contractors.

WORKING OUT COSTS – THE BUDGET

Writing down a clear budget before beginning will help to allow for those hidden extras later on as jobs often end up costing more than you expect. You may also wish to compare a number of different options.

For small changes the easiest way is to contact the necessary suppliers to find out prices. Check whether the figure includes VAT and delivery. For a more complex job, make a spreadsheet to itemize each material, the labour costs and the contingency. Materials are generally priced per square metre so measure the area that you will be covering. Even if you are just painting your house, work out the surface area to be covered before buying paint. Use your scale drawing or make a rough estimate from your sketch. Multiply the quantity by the unit price to get the cost. Phone at least two suppliers for each item to get a price comparison and do not forget to add in an amount for extras like fixings and scaffolding.

If using workmen, estimate labour costs by talking to the relevant contractors. You could use a single contractor to manage the project who will supply you with a total cost for work and materials. This is certainly easier but often more expensive. If you are undertaking a big scheme and you have little experience of construction then we would recommend that you do this; it may be more cost-effective in the long run.

Finally do not forget to add on a contingency cost of between five and ten per cent of the total costs for all those unexpected extras that are bound to crop up along the way.

When you have finished the quote you may wish to go back and modify a few items to reduce the costs. Make sure that any changes are made before you begin work because this will save a lot of unseen costs and wasted time after the construction work has begun.

MANAGING A PROJECT

If you feel that you are up to the challenge, you will save money by managing the project yourself. Your decision will depend on the size of the job, your own experience and knowledge, and your stress levels. Perhaps you want to stagger the works, get involved a little yourself and take your time.

Here are some useful pointers to successful project managing:
- Source all materials fully before starting any work.
- Think about what specialists you may need: engineers, architects, designers, surveyors and landscape designers. Ask for help where you need it, and don't expect to do everything yourself.
- Ensure that any permissions have been received before starting.
- Tie down any contractors with dates and costs.
- Get the site prepared as far as possible before any contractors arrive.
- Consider safety aspects for all involved.
- Maintain an activity chart showing the overall timescale, when any subcontractors will be on site and what order they need to work in. This will help you prevent any overlaps that may slow you down, such as contractors arriving for the next stage before the previous stage has been completed.
- Think about the details. For example, if you have rendered part of your building and wish to paint it, you will need to allow time for the render to dry first.
- Develop good working relationships. Once you hire a contractor you are at their mercy!
- Always try to think laterally and keep calm.
- Be realistic about your time and the time it will take to complete the project.
- Don't be afraid to seek advice from builders' merchants, hardware stores, reclamation yards, the Internet, books and magazines, or specialist companies.

FINDING CONTRACTORS

Personal recommendation is always the best way to find a contractor; responding to advertisements or going through telephone books can land you in tricky situations, although there are many good builders listed there. Always get references from any contractor or workman – it saves time in the long run to make a few phone calls or visit some of their previous jobs.

There are also different governing bodies that regulate standards and will give you advice, recommend contractors and will also check to see if a particular person is registered with them. Some examples of useful authorities are listed in Resources, pages 155–157.

Get several quotes from different builders, bearing in mind that the cheapest quote may not be the most realistic. Try to get the builders to do a breakdown of costs so you can compare like for like. Also ask for their day rates so that if extra work is necessary you have an idea of what you are likely to pay.

It is helpful to have some form of contract between you and the builder even if in the form of a letter. There are some good building resource stores that sell contracts for homeowners and can provide you with advice. It is also worth getting an end-date agreed, with some kind of penalty if the work goes over (and possibly a bonus if it finishes ahead of schedule). Some subcontractors such as window suppliers or electricians should give guarantees both for the materials and the workmanship.

Always communicate clearly with contractors – vague instructions will lead to problems with the work and the relationship you have with them.

BUILDING MATERIALS AND WORKMANSHIP

When thinking about materials to use you may wish to be adventurous. This is fine, but do consider the following factors before going ahead:

- The materials should be of a suitable nature and quality in relation to the purpose and conditions of their use.
- The materials must be mixed or prepared correctly.
- The materials must be applied, fixed or used so as to perform the functions for which they were intended.

An experienced builder or the material's manufacturer will often be able to advise you on the suitability of a material for a chosen application and its expected lifespan and maintenance requirements.

DOES IT ADD VALUE TO YOUR HOME?

If you are concerned about the value of your home, it may be worth discussing dramatic design plans with a local estate agent. Although renovating a property can add value, if a design is overly personalized it may not suit everyone and will narrow down the market for your property. On the other hand, if your design is particularly notable then it may make the property much more desirable. If you are undertaking works in order to add value then weigh up the investment costs against the potential increase in value. Take time to understand your market. Well-presented, newly painted, individual front doors and timber windows are all attractive elements to a potential buyer.

STRUCTURAL AND SURFACE PROBLEMS

Before starting a project make sure you study your building for any problems.

It is vital that you deal with these before you undertake anything on your wish list. Problems to watch for can include damp, settlement cracks, render/brickwork cracks, poor grouting in brickwork, rotten timber, loose tiles, poor insulation, condensation and water ingress.

In older properties, some 'defects' might only need attention if they are structurally dangerous or allow damp penetration. Defects may have been caused by slight subsidence which has since stopped or is progressive. Assess the urgency of the problem – a leaking roof will need immediate attention, but a flaking wall or an old settlement crack could be left for longer. Expert advice should always be sought if there is any doubt, and you might need a specialist to identify the correct treatment. Some architects and surveyors specialize in the renovation of old buildings and will advise whether a structural engineer is needed. They will also know the best firms or local craftsmen.

DAMP PROBLEMS

Gutters and downpipes are a common cause of damp. Check them to make sure they are sound, that the gutters have the right slope and are free from rubbish. Where downpipes discharge into an open gully at the base of the building, this should be cleaned out at least annually.

Blocked airbricks stop under-floor ventilation, causing dry rot in floor timbers, so keep them clear of earth and plants.

Damp, especially from behind a wall, removes paint surfaces, and is often the result of a non-existent or defective damp-proof course. This should be 150mm (5.9in) above the ground and render should be no lower as this could provide a bridge for the damp. Any adjacent paving should slope to drain away from the wall.

A different type of damp can occur on surfaces that are overhung by trees. It is essential that organic growth be treated with a suitable fungicide otherwise it will recur under any new decoration. Any loose material should be removed and weak and dusty surfaces treated with a stabilizing solution after thorough cleaning prior to decoration.

Far left: When paint starts coming off windows, the timber is exposed to the elements and will wear and rot. Remove the old paintwork and repair the wood before repainting with the correct paint.

Left: This cladding may have once formed a protective covering for the brickwork, but has cracked, possibly due to movement or settlement of the façade. Seek expect advice if you have any concerns.

REPAIRING ORIGINAL FEATURES

Your house may once have had plasterwork ornamentations that are damaged or have fallen off. If you wish to restore these features, look at the surrounding houses to see how they were originally used and then contact a skilled specialist. Some reproduction plaster mouldings can be bought from specialist companies.

Split or rotting timber cladding should be replaced with matching sections. When replacing the timber, always treat with a timber preservative and not varnish. You can then decide if you wish to paint the boards.

Walls

Stone or brick walls may need re-pointing. Rake the joints out by 2.5 cm/½ inch and then point them with appropriate cement using a 1:2:8 mortar mix, coloured if required. Old houses would generally have used white lime, so white cement in the mortar will match this. If you have damaged stonework, seek advice before cleaning. If replacing stone, try to match it with a similar stone and then re-point in the same method as for brickwork.

Renders, such as stucco or pebbledash, can be applied to waterproof a wall or disguise poor facing materials. Rendering can be stripped off or protected (see Cladding, pages 83–90). Fill fine cracks with a mixture of masonry paint and Portland cement, worked well in, then smoothed down. Rough renderings are commonly known as dry dash, which is hard to clean and repair. If it needs to be patched, use rendering that will have a similar texture – patchy render looks terrible.

Metalwork

Examine and clean iron and other metals in railings, gutters, downpipes and door furniture. Rusty areas should be wire-brushed and treated with a rust inhibitor, followed by an appropriate paint. Fill in open joints or cracks with lead putty. Bare spots can be touched up with zinc or calcium plumbate primer. The insides of metal gutters should be painted with two coats of bituminous paint or another anti-corrosive coating.

Windows

Check timber windows and doors for rot and replace any defective sections. Clean out drip grooves under the sills and opening windows and doors. Make sure that the vulnerable top edges are painted since they are often overlooked. Bare timber sills and thresholds need to be liberally oiled. Joints can be filled with non-setting mastic, which lets the timbers move. Check metal windows for rusting.

External issues

Ivy or other climbing plants can cause cracking and damage. Check planting regularly to make sure it is not creeping into places it shouldn't. Lead flashing can also crack and cause damp penetration. Pointing and flashing should be checked and replaced if necessary.

CHAPTER SUMMARY

The quality of the job lies with the individual carrying out the work. The cheapest job is often the least economic in the long run – the contractor may not have taken into account all the potential difficulties of the job, and inevitably you will end up paying for it. So do a lot of research and planning, discuss the work with a number of contractors and agree a fee that seems reasonable for the amount of work to be carried out. This will give you the most important element needed before embarking on a project – peace of mind.

CHAPTER 3
ENTRANCES: DOORS AND PORCHES

The front door is generally where a visitor pauses and looks around before entering a house. Think about your house for a moment: the front door greets you every day when you come home, the porch is where you welcome your guests, and most importantly the doorway is the first part of your home that you have a tactile relationship with. In addition, this is the threshold that takes you from the street or front garden into the interior environment of your house. Therefore it is essential to consider all the aspects that make up your entrance way, from the doorbell to the letterbox to the handle and even the front step. Each item within the entrance will influence the first impressions of any guest and has the potential to make your house a pleasure to come home to.

FRONT DOORS

The most important feature of any house is the front door. It is the welcome sign that you give to every visitor who approaches your home and the first point of physical contact with the house.

Have you considered the look, the colour, the transparency, the size, or even the position of your front door? How does the door appear in relation to the rest of the house? Is it defined, accentuated with a surround? Is it difficult to notice from the street, concealed down the side of the house? Has it been altered in some way from when it was first built? What does the door say about you, your family and your lifestyle?

The appearance of the door is often overlooked. Some are more inviting than others, some fit comfortably with the overall look of the house, while others do not entice you to go any further than the garden gate.

So what turns a front door into an appealing entrance? How can you personalize the door so that it gives the right message to friends and strangers? Can the front door be linked in some way to the interior? Whatever you decide to do with your front door will be of great significance to the impression of the house.

The Christian tradition is to adorn the front door with a wreath of holly at Christmas – based on the pagan ritual of warding off evil spirits. Hindus decorate the front door with mango leaves up to two days before a wedding. These remain there until the first wedding anniversary. The door is also decorated at the festival of Divali (see page 17).

WHAT IMPRESSION DO YOU WANT TO GIVE?

Rather than begin with the practical side of choosing a door, it is worth considering the personal aspects important to you:

- How can you make your door inviting?
- Do you want it to be individual?
- Should it fit in with the historic style of the house and/or match other doors in the neighbourhood?
- What colours do you find welcoming?
- What is the colour scheme of your house?
- Do you want a contemporary, individualized front door that reflects your character?
- Do you want your door to let light in to your hall?
- Do you need to see people arrive for security/other purposes?
- Does your door need solidity and weight for security purposes?

Walk around your neighbourhood and make a note of the entrances that you like and those that you do not. Look at their different components. They might consist of:

- The porch
- The front door
- The letterbox
- The doorbell
- The house number
- Door step and mat
- A storage space for recycling, outdoor shoes etc.
- Lighting

Think about what you like and try to define it; for example, 'the bright-coloured door with no glass panel', rather than just 'Mrs Smith's front door'.

WHICH FRONT DOOR WILL BEST SUIT YOUR HOUSE?

Front doors take many shapes, forms, colours and materials. You may wish to retain the original front door if your house has a distinct architectural design or find out what style of door your house would have had when first built. The type of original door will depend on the era that the house was built in and its style and size. Have a look at neighbouring houses to see if they have their original doors, or at archive photo-graphs of your house and street. This can help identify the original design concept, which can either be worked in to your vision or be completely recreated. Alternatively you could change your door to a new design – traditional or contemporary.

Classic influence

Georgian front doors and surrounds were generally based on Greek or Roman architecture. They tended to be plain, made from solid panels and with no ornamentation. A classical portico may have been built over the door, but most doors were seen as part of the whole elevation in terms of proportion. There may have been a glass panel above the door to allow light into the hallway.

Victorian entrances were given more dominance and decoration. The top two panels in the door often contained leaded, coloured glass that had been hand-blown and made up using small pieces. Imposing decorative surrounds emphasized the importance of the resident within. Inspiration for the designs was taken from the Italian Renaissance and, later, the Gothic revival. This was characterized by rounded or pointed arches and decorated columns in plasterwork. Georgian and Victorian front doors were always painted, usually in dark colours such as black, brown, maroon, or dark green.

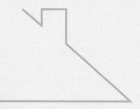

RESTRICTIONS ON DOORS
In England and Wales, there are three grades of listing: Grade I, Grade II* and Grade II. If your property is Grade I or Grade II* listed, you need to get consent from English Heritage for any changes you wish to make to your front door. If your house is Grade II listed or in a Conservation Area, and has an Article 4 Directive (these are zones that have been allocated as protected in some way by the planning department), you are obliged to contact the council to get the requested changes approved. It is always worth checking before starting any kind of work by telephoning your local planning department.

Traditional style

During the Edwardian era, design was influenced by the Arts and Crafts movement, and sought to bring a greater sense of nature and the country-side back into house design. There was a renewed interest in traditional crafts which is most clearly seen in the designs of the glass panelling in the front door. The surrounds to the door were less ornate, often with a simple porch supported using curved or simply-styled timber beams.

Art Nouveau was a movement that was defined as taking its inspiration from nature – flowers, leaves and other long, swirling decorative and organic forms, as seen in the work of Charles Rennie Mackintosh. His ornate designs were used in glass panelling set into doors, fretwork and detailing of supports both inside and out.

Jacobethan was the style at the turn of the century that most reflected the rural cottage. The idea was to frame and emphasize the door, which was ideally composed of oak studs with false nail heads and strap hinges, sturdy enough to give the impression of solidity and cosiness. Alternatively, the door had six small glass panels arranged in a rectangular or oval pattern in the top third of the door. A porch was an essential part of the door to aid this sense of escape from the elements.

Twentieth-century designs

After World War II, there were a number of movements that were inspired by the new advances in technology – for the first time design stopped looking to the past and now looked to the future. The Art Deco movement took speed and travel as its defining style and was inspired by Aztec and Mayan art in South American and Egyptian pyramids, as well as the art movements of Cubism and Futurism. The lines and forms of the Art Deco style are very clearly defined – jagged shapes, zigzag lines and straight geometrical designs. Exterior domestic applications of the style are seen in leaded glass panels, garage doors and gates.

Symbols of the machine age such as ocean liners, cars and aeroplanes were also used in architectural design. Doors often reflected this with full-length windows inset into the door or a plain cantilevered porch over a flush-panelled, black-painted door; the porch itself may have had a porthole or diamond-shaped window.

Another popular fashion was the Sunspan house, where the idea was to get as much sun as possible inside. Sunbeam designs were incorporated into the glazing of the door and the patterning of the front gates. Later styles included adding a wrought iron grille with stylized ivy leaf patterns over the full-length glazing panel in the front door.

PRACTICAL CONSIDERATIONS

Once you have some idea of the possible style of door, it is time to think about the more practical aspects, including your budget and security considerations. This may narrow down your selection somewhat. This checklist will ensure that your entrance will be both functional and individual. The points are all discussed in greater detail later, but you will need to consider:

- **The size of the opening.** Is your door large enough for you, the shopping, the buggy, the bicycle, the deliveries and the kids? Building Regulations state that a new door must be wide enough to allow a wheelchair to access the interior – the recommended clearance is 800mm (31.5in) wide with a 13mm (0.5in) lip at the threshold.
- **The door furniture.** This includes all the additions to the door that make it possible to open and close the door freely. You may need some or all of the following: hinges, door knobs and handles, locking mechanisms, letterbox, spyhole, door closers and door number.

- **The vision panel.** How solid a front door do you want? How public or private do you want your entrance to be? Think about how much natural light you wish to get into the hallway. For security purposes, most people want some way of seeing the person at the door before opening it, but at the same time perhaps you do not want everyone to see directly inside your home.
- **Security.** Decide on the functional aspects and what your insurance policy requires for the locking mechanisms and hinges.
- **Draft excluders.** With every opening made in a wall it is important to create strong seals around all the edges to prevent water and wind from penetrating the building.

And last but not least:
- **Budget.** How much is it all going to cost you? Make sure you include the cost of fittings and trimmings as they quickly add up.

IDENTIFYING TYPES OF MATERIALS

Choosing the right type of material for your door is the next step. Today, commonly used materials for doors are wood or PVC, although doors can be made from any secure and weatherproof material. There are advantages and disadvantages to both wood and PVC, so it is important to find the door that suits you and your house.

Wood

A wooden door looks substantial and textured, but will need maintenance. Doors come in either hardwood or softwood and the cost reflects the type. For an exterior door, it is best to use a hardwood which, if maintained, will last for many years – it is not unusual to find wooden doors that are hundreds of years old that are still in perfect condition. Commonly used timbers are meranti, oak or mahogany. If using hardwood, make sure the timber is Forest Stewardship Council (FSC) certified. If a softwood is used then ensure it is a solid core door. Always check with the supplier what the door consists of (i.e. whether it is made of a sandwich of different timbers).

The door should be painted or sealed on a regular basis – the paintwork on a good quality, new wooden door is often guaranteed for approximately eight years. As a rule of thumb, re-paint or seal the door before it shows significant signs of wear and tear. The great advantage of this type of door is that you can change its colour as often as you like. You can expose the wood of a solid hardwood door but it needs to be oiled or lacquered. Oiling the door needs to be done regularly and will bring up the natural grain of the timber. Be careful to test the lacquer on the wood first as some finishes can make the wood look like it has a plastic coating.

UPVC

To avoid the hassle of maintaining a door, you may wish to install one made of PolyVinyl Chloride (PVC) or Unplasticized PolyVinyl Chloride (UPVC). The most widely used of all plastics, UPVC will not warp, rot or discolour and never needs painting (which means virtually no maintenance). This is a highly insulate material and can be extremely hard-wearing. Though these doors can provide the illusion of a wooden door, they lack character and texture and are generally quite unattractive. They do not age, which will mean that the door will stand out from the rest of the materials of the house such as the brickwork, which will wear and provide character to your home over time. UPVC doors are available in a very limited colour palette and you cannot paint them, which can be very restricting if you ever want to change the look of your house. They also have an intricate frame and hinge system designed so that you can only replace like for like. Because they are lightweight, they can also feel flimsy to the touch. In addition UPVC is more harmful to the environment, both in its production and when it is disposed of as it is difficult to recycle and is generally thrown into a landfill site.

Many of the houses featured in *Front of House* had UPVC doors, which were difficult to alter. One way to overcome this was simply to clad the door in a thin sheet of 10mm (½in) external grade plywood that could then be painted, scored with lines or decorated.

Other materials

Aluminium doors can replicate most timber styles. They are similar in most respects to UPVC, but have the advantage of being stronger. Composite doors that have a core of aluminium and a cladding of timber are also available. Another possibility is a high-security steel door constructed from a steel body with a thin layer of wood cladding. All these are mass-produced items and there is a range of styles available for you to choose from.

Finally, it is worth considering cladding the door. In the Art Deco period of the 1920s, metal cladding became fashionable for doors and other areas of a building. Brass, copper, galvanized steel and aluminium are all examples of sheet metals that could be used to create a more unusual effect by cladding the timber frame of a front door.

To summarize, wooden doors improve with age and provide the flexibility to be adapted, whereas UPVC only degrade with time. Wood will have a greater sense of appropriateness with the architecture of a home than UPVC. Doors can vary greatly in design, so you should not feel limited to use only styles that are readily available – it is easy to create your own design.

TYPES OF DOOR

Most mass-produced doors come in standardized sizes, so if you are on a budget then it is worth consulting a brochure from a large door supplier to see if there are any types that would suit your requirements. The following is a list of some of the types of doors available:

- Panel doors.
- Doors with glass panels.
- Doors with leaded lights.
- Solid doors. These are available in a tongue-and-grooved style to look like an industrial farm door.
- Half-doors or stable doors. These are where the top half opens independently from the bottom half and were used in the past to open a part of the door while preventing animals from entering.
- Fire check doors. Only necessary if you live in a shared flat with a common entrance.
- Double doors. Sometimes present in a larger house.
- French doors. If your social garden space happens to be in the front of your house then you might wish to think carefully about the appearance of the front door.

CREATING INDIVIDUALITY

You should now have some idea of what you need, want and can afford for your new front door, so it's time to get creative! Beyond a door providing the entrance to a house, there are no rules about its potential design. If you're not confident in your artistic abilities, you may wish to find an artist who can produce a design for your door. Wooden doors can be treated as a canvas to be painted and treated in various ways. Consider techniques that were used on the door for Zoe Tune (see page 44) or other possible techniques such as scorching the wood, punching holes and filling with different materials,

painting stripes, layering stains and varnishes, changing the shape of glazed areas or adding new glazed areas. It is not always necessary to consider glass as the only material for vision panels, as different effects can be created using a multitude of materials. Polycarbonate or perspex, for instance, comes in a variety of designs and colours. The main thing to remember is that whatever treatment you give to the door, it must remain weatherproof.

DOOR TERMINOLOGY

External door frame. This is the wooden frame that fits into the hole in the external wall, on to which the door is hung. Door frames should be made of sound external-grade wood or another externally durable material and securely bolted or screwed to the wall every 60cm (23.6in) around the whole frame.

Door casing. This is the decorative framing around a door or window. It may be used on its own, or in conjunction with an over-door ornament.

Door lining. This is the section within the door frame that stops the door from coming back on itself. Door linings can be rebated for intumescent or smoke seal strips.

Intumescent strip. This is a PVC profile that, under the action of heat such as a fire, will soften as the intumescent material within it expands and seals the gap between the door and frame. These strips are placed on doors to a fire escape route such as a corridor in a house or a common escape corridor to some flats, and will isolate a fire to a particular room. If you are unsure about using these strips, consult a door supplier.

CASE STUDY
Zoe Tune's front door

The design of Zoe Tune's house uses the front door as the central inspiration for the rest of the house. The door has been reclaimed from a salvage yard and was then cut to size to fit Zoe's door opening. Oliver worked on the door, initially with a blow torch to scorch it to bring up the grain, and then painted a series of horizontal stripes in various colours on to it. Other techniques for applying graphics to the door could be to make a stencil (perhaps from a photograph), to paint on a sequence of repeated images or to use a special transfer paper to put a photographic image on to the door. Alternatively, tonal shades of paint could be splattered on to the door, or text written or stencilled on in order to individualize it. Your front door really is an opportunity to use your imagination, especially if you are willing to move away from the conventional notion of what a front door should look like.

The inspiration for Zoe's door was then projected on to the rest of the house, which was mainly designed to be a large graphic that covered the entire façade. The theme of circles and lines were applied using a limited palette of colours on to a background pale green. The theme was also carried through to the garden fence and gate (see page 94). The final result was a house with an abstract, but modern, appearance that livened up the street.

Colours

The colour of a door can very effectively set a mood. During the reign of Queen Victoria, English houses were notoriously fronted by black painted doors. This was seen a mark of respect for the Queen while she was in mourning for Albert. In Ireland, this decree by the Queen of England had the opposite effect of creating a landscape of brightly coloured doors. Look at the colour of your door in relation to the rest of the house. You may wish to contrast the façade with the door, to highlight one or the other, or to complement it with the colour of other external features.

Made to measure

You may wish to specify the exact design of a door to a joiner who will be able to fabricate the door for you. This can work out to be quite expensive and it is important to find a joiner who is experienced in making doors. In addition, if you are measuring up the door then there needs to be an allowance for the timber to move. Most timbers will expand when wet and shrink when dry, though the amount varies depending on what type of wood you use. You must take this into account when measuring the door to fit so that that the door does not jam in the winter. Any good joiner will be able to advise you on this.

GETTING A PREMIER FINISH

Number 10, Downing Street is one of the most famous front doors in the world, and it has an immaculate paint finish. To achieve this finish takes a lot of hard work. The door must be prepared so that all imperfections are filled and sanded until completely smooth. Apply an undercoat with a good quality brush and then apply several layers of top coat. Between each application, rub down the paintwork with fine-grade sandpaper to maintain the smooth surface. A product called Obertrawl (or linseed oil) can also be added to the top coat; this thins the paint so that it applies very evenly. Most thinners such as white spirit actually work against the natural make-up of oil-based paints by weakening the structure, whereas this product thins the paint whilst maintaining the quality of the oil-based structure and improving the finish.

Vision panels

Doors will often include some glazing to bring light into the hallway and for security purposes. Some doors have vision panels, which is glazing at the side of the door. This can help let more light into the property and add a design feature. For example, look at how glass has been used in this image of a door from the Art Nouveau period.

At the turn of the 20th century it was usual for the hall to be lit by an extra window by the front door in the form of a small oriel or porthole glazed with stained glass. Stained glass and leadwork are typical decorative elements of front doors.

Modern front doors often have much larger sections of glazing. In some cases the door is all glass with a small frame surround. All external doors that have more than a 50 per cent glazed area, including the frame, must comply with Building Regulations to maintain energy efficiency by reducing heat losses and introducing much higher standards of insulation.

The Window Openings chapter (see pages 56–75) contains plenty of advice on glass types and glazing techniques as well as explanations of Building Regulations connected with glass.

Recycled doors

Doors are regularly salvaged from old buildings and can provide a beautiful addition to an old house, as well as increasing the property's value by adding an original feature. The best way to find old doors is to visit reclamation yards. Make sure you find a door that fits – reclaimed doors do not come in standard sizes. Door frames can be adjusted slightly by a joiner, as can a door that is slightly too large, but a door that is too small cannot be made bigger.

When you have chosen a suitable door of the correct size and desired style, make sure that it is not warped. Warping occurs when the woodwork of a door becomes saturated with water, either through worn paintwork or a leak running through to the frame. Once a door is warped it will not fit the door frame snugly and can leak or become draughty. (It is possible to dry a warped door until it is back to its original shape but this process can take a long time.) When reclaiming a door there are many treatments that you can apply to change its existing look. You may wish to strip the original paintwork, which can be done very simply before the door is hung by dipping it in a special acid; alternatively, paintwork can be removed with a blowtorch and a scraper. Never strip a door unless it is made of oak or a similar hardwood and therefore designed to be varnished – stripped doors are rare and usually found in Arts and Crafts houses from the Art Nouveau period.

The lines of the door structure have been broken by the curved lines of the glazing to either side.

DOOR FURNITURE

Choosing the right door furniture requires time, as it can say a lot about the owners and has an impact on security. Door furniture provides a visitor with the initial physical contact with the house, so it should feel solid and confident to the touch. Choose materials that will look good and fit in with the look of the house.

HINGES

A typical front door hinges on one side and opens inwards, but there are exceptions, such as double doors that open centrally. Ensure that the hinge is made of a non-combustible material that meets British Standards. Hinges made of mazak and aluminium are not suitable – you need a material that will not rust and that will support the door, such as steel, brass or phosphor bronze. Most hinges are concealed so it is hard to hang a door well; if you are worried, ask a joiner or carpenter.

SECURITY

To meet the requirements of insurance companies, your front door should be fitted with a rim latch (Yale type) and a mortice deadlock (commonly five-lever), or at least a rim automatic deadlock. Both must be to BS 3621 or the equivalent European Standard EN12209.

Even with these locks, security also depends on the door and door frame. Both must be suitable for external use so, for example, a wooden door with a hollow core would not be appropriate. Doors should be at least 45mm (1¾in) thick and should be hung on three strong hinges to support the lock, which should be fitted 45 to 60cm (18 to 23½in) from the latch.

Recessed or decorative panels should be at least 10mm (⅜in) thick. You could also fit a London bar (a metal strip on the frame side) to support the strike box (which takes the latch), or a Birmingham bar to support the frame on the hinge side. If the door is weak, you can fit a sheet steel plate or door reinforcer on the outside to cover the lock area.

A door with a glazed area will be less secure than a solid door. To improve security, use laminated glass (two pieces of glass held together with a sheet of laminate) or Georgian wired glass – these are much more resistant to breakage.

You may wish to fit a viewer to allow you to see who is outside, and a door chain or limiter. These are available from any good locksmith or hardware store.

UPVC front doors are generally unsuitable for additional security devices as the material is not strong enough to support them, and changes to the original design may invalidate the warranty or damage the integral locking assembly. If in doubt, consult the installer/manufacturer. Modern designs usually incorporate deadlock shoot bolts or a multi-point locking system, both throwing a number of bolts from the door into the frame.

Letterbox security

Letterboxes can be used by criminals to access goods inside a door or to work locking devices from the inside. They should be positioned at least 40cm (15 ½in) from the door lock and never to the bottom rail of the door. An internal cover plate and a letter basket offer extra security, though you might wish to remove the bottom of a basket to allow mail to fall to the floor, thus preventing theft. If you are worried about whether access through the letterbox is a possibility, you could add extra locks such as draw bolts to the inside.

IRONMONGERY, DOORBELL AND LETTERBOX

A typical door will have a letterbox, a bell or knocker (or both) and a handle or knob. These are the tactile elements of the door and therefore it is worth considering the form of the handle and the material from which it is made. As with hinges, door furniture comes in many types of metal finishes and there are plenty of standard products on the market that replicate traditional styles, as well as companies that specialize in more contemporary items. See Resources (pages 155–157) for stockists. You can also try going to salvage yards for unusual door knockers. Door furniture is a simple way to express some personality on to your house.

Doorbells come in a variety of designs with different rings and mechanisms – even small details make an impression, which is often greater than you might expect. Think about how it will look – do you want a round metal doorbell, or an unusual door knocker? We all remember the tune-playing doorbell!

DOOR NUMBER/HOUSE NAME

Your house is either named or numbered, or both. If you want to name your house or change its name, you need to apply to your local council. They will check with Royal Mail that the proposed name is not the same or similar to other properties in the same area. If you are given permission, you will be obliged to continue to use the door number as well and you will have to register the name with the Royal Mail's Address Management department. The council will supply a list of other organizations and departments for you to inform.

The tradition of putting lions, stone dogs or gargoyles either on to or in front of the door goes back to as early as medieval times. It was believed these would protect the owners of the house. Sometimes glass balls were hung above the door to ward off evil spirits of the pagan tradition.

Adding individuality

We are used to seeing a door number as metal plates screwed on to the face of the door, usually in brass or cast iron, but there are many other options for presenting a door number and house name. With a little imagination the door number can become a feature of your house.

Your house number or name does not necessarily need to be presented on the door. You could create an interesting graphic using the number and paint it on the house, or perhaps write out the number; for example, Thirty Five rather than 35. An interesting effect can be created quite simply and stylishly by handwriting the number and having it made up in neon light – this creates a very bold and confident statement which is certainly eye-catching and can look very effective on the right house (see page 105).

The door number/name could also be etched on to any glazed areas on the building or simply painted on to the door or a nearby surface. Ensure the number is large enough to be clearly visible. The etching can be done by having the graphic sandblasted into the glass or by simply applying a laminate film to the window (see page 66). Laminates come in a range of colours and finishes, such as opaque, translucent and metallic. For information on producing a laminate, contact your local graphic printer. When painting, it is worth using a stencil unless you are confident with a paintbrush.

Right: The inspiration for this seaside house was found in objects such as deck chairs, piers, amusement arcades, flags and bunting. The number is in lights and bright colours in the style of a funfair graphic, and was made by cutting out the number in exterior-grade plywood, painting it and drilling holes for lights. Ask a qualified electrician to install any lights for outside use.

Far right: The number for the Mediterranean house was part of the graphics painted on to the façade. The font and colour used matched the rest of the highlighted painted areas (see page 81). By drawing around a projected image, the number was traced on to the wall and then carefully filled in with paint.

Whether printed or painted, choose a font you like for the number/name. Every style of font will give a different image – you can choose from most of the fonts that appear on your word processing package in your computer. These range from a curvaceous traditional font to a sans serif font with minimal character.

For a contemporary feel, you can use modern materials such as brushed stainless steel. Even the detail of how the number is fitted to the wall can be important. Invisible fixtures can be used for fitting. These subtle differences to traditional fixtures will make all the difference to the impact.

In Britain, a number of quirky houses have been given their identity through the eccentric numbering or naming of the house. In some ways naming your house is like giving it a personality and an outward expression of yourself. The artists Gilbert and George renamed their house 'Eleven and a half' which they painted onto the door of a typical Georgian terrace house. The subtle change makes people look twice and then remember it – the front of your house should do the same.

MINI PROJECT Ideas for new ways to display the house number

1 Use projection such as in the Mediterranean house (see page 81) or Colonial house (see page 15) to display a number and then paint it.
2 Burnish letters or numbers into wood such as in the Beachcomber house (page 14) – get a blacksmith to help.
3 Use lighting to highlight the number, as above.
4 Etch film into the glazed window of your door (see the Boatbuilder house door, page 105).
5 Cut the numbers out into a metal sheet.
6 Have a light box made in vinyl, with the number highlighted.
7 Create a number in stained glass.

PORCHES

Whether a simple covered entrance to a home or a fully enclosed room on the outside of a building, a porch can dramatically alter the perception of your house.

It brings a focus to the façade and gives a physical sense of welcome and an opportunity for expression. It is especially useful in bad weather, and in some cases is used as a sun shade. The most common material for a porch is UPVC, but as discussed previously, this is a very difficult material to alter and often does not match the rest of the house. You may also have an existing porch which does not suit the house, in which case you may want to remove it or replace it with something more stylish.

Historically, porches were first introduced to liven up the flat Georgian façade. Regency houses were updated with wood, brick and stucco or stone porticoes, while Victorians generally moved their porches inside or turned them into a recess within the building. From around 1900, hoods over the front door were revived but usually in a picturesque cottage-style with timber gables, or red-tiled roofs supported on oak posts. Sometimes striped awnings were used to keep the sun from the door. Whatever the style, the common theme was that porches were never enclosed. Across the Atlantic, American houses often feature porches which function as an outside social and relaxation space, an idea which has become more popular over here.

PORCH POSSIBILITIES

If your house currently has a porch that seems out of keeping with your design you should not feel that it is necessary to work around this. A porch can be removed quite simply provided you have consent to do so if necessary. If in doubt, however, check with a builder, surveyor or engineer.

If you don't want to remove your porch completely, you could revamp the existing structure by changing the cladding materials. On Mark and Louise's house (see page 87), the 60s-style stone cladding, which today has connotations more of Coronation Street than anything else, was replaced by a slate cladding, which comes in small pieces like mosaic. The new finish is still a natural material but gives a simple block of colour and texture to the exterior to provide a contemporary feel.

It is also a good idea to incorporate lighting around the porch so that people can clearly see their way to the front door. This is discussed in more detail in the Lighting chapter, pages 96–113.

Before planning and building a porch you must first find out if you need to obtain building consent (see the section on planning restrictions, pages 25–26).

CHOOSING YOUR MATERIALS

With a bit of imagination, a porch could be made from nearly anything. Decide on the function that is required; whether it needs to enclosed all or part of the time, whether with openable windows or fixed screens. Will you use the porch as a sun room for additional sitting or just for shade? Do you want to store things in it – bicycles, coats and hats, or a baby's buggy? Can you build in an area to conceal your dustbins? You could also extend the use of your porch so that it becomes a place to separate your rubbish before recycling. This would mean an area for glass bottles, cans and paper.

Be careful of using bespoke porches that bear no resemblance to the rest of the house. Often it is best to use one or just two materials such as timber or a combination of timber and slate, to give a subtle aesthetic appeal.

THREE DIFFERENT PORCHES

Hazel's house (above left and page 102) was inspired by Edward Hopper. The existing porch, which was a PVC and glass box porch, was removed and in its place a printed retractable awning was hung which gives an otherwise very boxy house an added three-dimensionality. The awning gives a relaxed feel to the house and has influences of a 1930s French style.

On Julie's house (above centre and page 68), a small cantilevered concrete roof existed that was painted and then framed using reclaimed iron gates. The rust was sanded off and the gates welded together and repainted to give a delicate frame to the doorway. The property is small with tiny windows so adding a porch opens the house out and gives it a country-cottage feel.

A different porch was created for Elaine's house (otherwise known as the Mediterranean house, above right and page 152), using a stacking effect of timber planters either side of the door which were filled with scented plants. This porch appeals to our sense of smell and affects every entry and exit to this home in a subtle yet memorable way.

CASE STUDY
A Rock 'n' Roll porch

All of the designs for *Front of House* were drawn with the individual characters and interests of the occupants in mind. The house that became known as the 'Rock 'n' Roll' house is occupied by a young couple, Jason and Kate, one of whom plays in a band. Their attitude was open and fresh and their only direct specification was that they wanted the house to appear more three-dimensional.

It was therefore decided to make a dramatic statement with the porch. The overall square shape of the house was broken by using a circular opening in relief from the house. The circle has associations with the shape of a record or CD, referencing the music theme. It gives the house a sense of fun – almost as though it should belong in an Austin Powers movie. The bright red colour used on the inside of the porch highlights the shape and draws attention to the doorway – portal to another dimension!

The face on to which the porch has been attached has been given a very smooth render and painted light grey so that the circular form of the porch protrudes in a clearly defined way from its background. The face of the house has also been broken up with an area of slate and a section of shiplap timber cladding. The natural materials and grey render give the look of a modernist design which is disrupted by a burst of colour inside the porch. The association with the colour red can also be likened to the 'red carpet'.

A side gate was made to reflect the design of the porch (see also page 54). This was built from semi-translucent frosted acrylic attached to a metal framework. The framework, which is subtly visible through the perspex, also has a metal circle the size of the porch welded on to the gate. The circle also acts as part of the structure for the gate. The frosting of the acrylic gives privacy to the driveway and a sense of security.

FRONT STEPS

You can do more to your front step than simply placing a welcome mat or a couple of paving stones. This area is as important as the front door but is often overlooked.

The detail at the base of the front door is known as the threshold. For disabled access it is important that the entrance threshold is ramped, a legal requirement for all new homes. The step demarks a territory that separates your private domain from the public one, and is even more important in houses that do not have front gardens. In blocks of flats you can often see people lining the floor area in front of their door with tiles or a mat to show the edge of the entrance to the house.

IMAGINATIVE USES

A number of different materials have been used to make new front doorsteps for *Front of House*. For Barry and Kerry's house (see page 84 and below), the step was made in timber as a box and then raised slightly off ground level. A waterproof light was placed beneath the step so that at night the step appeared to hover above the ground. It is important to remember to use timber with grooves in it to prevent the surface from becoming slippery.

Another idea for cladding a step is to use mosaics. These can be used in a variety of colours by breaking up old tiles or pieces of mirror. The grout used for this should not be smooth so that a slip-resistance is created. This can be a great project for personalizing an entrance and is easy to do, if a bit time-consuming.

For a change in structure, try using a metal grating or structural glass set into a metal frame. These need to be constructed for you. The glass can be etched with the house number to give it a slip-resistance. If you want to use these materials, it is important to get the detail and specification right so talk to an architect or manufacturer. The glass step could be back-lit to give a glowing effect at night.

Barry and Kerry's front door adds to the colourful, modern, 'stylistic' house. A glowing overhead perspex porch was added and an elongated step underlit to 'hover' at night.

GARAGE DOORS AND CAR PORTS

When car ownership became common in the late 1930s, houses began to be constructed with built-in garages. Today, houses often have a garage or space for a car on one side of the property.

It is not always necessary to enclose the garage in order to provide protection for the car; a roof covering can be added as a car port. If you are thinking of building a garage, always check whether you need planning permission before starting. It is also worth speaking to your neighbours. Most building work is quite complicated, so ensure that you do your research first.

DESIGN CONSIDERATIONS

If you have a garage that is visible from the front of your house, try to create a design that integrates both. If you need to park your car in the front driveway of your house, this should be considered in the design. Chris Webb, the owner of the 'England with a twist' house (see page 20), had several cars parked in the front drive, which created a jumbled look. As a special design feature of this property, a high solid gate was added to the side of the house, behind which the cars could be parked and hidden from view. The gate also extends the front face of the building, which makes the house look larger and gives the whole façade a defined appearance.

It is most appealing if the garage door can be colour-coded with the front of the house, the front door or some other feature.

It may also be possible to clad doors to the garage with wood or metal mesh. Make sure the fixings are secure and long-lasting as the door needs to open and close often. Try to stencil on the house number, paint on a graphic image or some text. Just have some fun!

Far left: In Lolly's house, the colours that were used for the façade were painted as stripes on the garage door to tie the garage in with the rest of the house rather than have it as a separate feature.

Left: Jason and Kate's garage door is the third circle in the theme – linking it to the front porch and the driveway which also feature circles (see page 52). It is made of etched Perspex that has been fixed on to a welded metal frame door.

ENTRANCES DOS AND DON'TS

DO
- Decide on the entire scheme before beginning on a small part of it. This means taking into account your budget, your requirements and your design. See if you can add some unique qualities to your property while still maintaining an overall harmony.
- Use timber front doors where possible as they provide creative freedom.
- Design your own porch or re-clad an existing inappropriate one.
- Liven up the front doorstep.
- Change the appearance of your door number to reflect your home, your interests and your lifestyle.
- Tie in the garage door to any new design changes that you have for your front door.
- Consult recommended builders to help you with any construction works.

DON'T
- Use PVC if you wish to make alterations or creative additions to your door.
- Follow through on only half the idea, such as building a plastic porch that does not reflect the house style or making a beautiful new front door that cannot be seen clearly.
- Do any building works – either removing or replacing – without first checking with the relevant authority whether you have permission to do so.
- Forget to use the correct number of coats of paint and sealants for exterior conditions.
- Attempt to do any building work that you are unsure about – a bad job on something as important as your front door will cause a good deal of grief in the long term.

CHAPTER 4
WINDOW OPENINGS AND ACCESSORIES

In this chapter we will explain the main issues relating to windows. We will pay particular attention to what you can do to modify your existing window openings with simplicity and ease. In this way both their appearance and function can be altered to suit your requirements. If you are thinking about making major changes – changing the window or creating new openings, for example – we suggest you discuss your plans first with an architect, who can give you detailed advice about the procedure as well as help you to visualize the design.

WINDOWS

A window can be thought of as having two different faces: an outside one connecting with the exterior of the house and an inside one that links with the interior.

Each side has different criteria to satisfy, often with conflicting demands. The exterior side of the window is part of the appearance of your house. It breaks up the often-flat façade of the exterior wall, giving a proportion and scale to the house, and adding character and style. On the interior face of the window, a different set of priorities are important. The size, openness and orientation of the window will dictate the amount of light entering the property as well as the level of ventilation in it.

TAKING A FRESH LOOK AT YOUR HOUSE

To begin with, look at the façade of the house from both the outside and the inside. Ask yourself the following questions:

General appearance
- What do the windows add to the façade ?
- Are they distinct, styled or anonymous?
- What type of windows are they?
- What materials are they made from?
- What condition are the window frames in?
- Have they been changed from the original?

Impressions
- What do other people see when they look at my house?
- Can they see into the interior or can they just see the net curtains?
- How does the appearance differ when the curtains are open and when they are closed?
- Are the windows friendly, inviting and soft or do they make my house look hard and severe?
- Are there security bars?

Light
- How much light enters the room?
- Are there obstacles such as curtains or exterior planting that prevent light from entering inside?
- Is there too much direct sunlight coming in?

Aspect
- What is the view out of the room?
- How often do I look out of the window?
- How important is it to have a view?
- How visible am I?
- Do I mind if people can see in?
- Do I feel secure?

Practical considerations
- How much colder is it close up to the window?
- Can I hear and feel the wind blowing through the window?
- Is there any condensation on the inside of the window?
- What is the temperature like in the room?
- Is the room noisy?
- Is the room stuffy?
- Can I open the window?
- How does the window define the interior?
- What colour are the windows on both the inside and out?

Once you have defined the positive and negative aspects of your windows you are in a clearer position to make some decisions as to what type of changes need to be made: replacing the existing windows; creating new openings; or simply making alterations by the addition of accessories, and painting externally and/or internally.

Planting can be attractive on the exterior of your house, but take care that it is not to the detriment of the light levels in the interior. Cut back the planting and let the light flood in.

WHAT DO YOUR WINDOWS SAY ABOUT YOU?

A street elevation is made up of many windows, each reflecting a person's lifestyle, habits and tastes. We all have a tendency to look at houses when we walk down the street to get clues as to who lives in our neighbourhood. What types of people share our street with us? An undressed window might suggest an occupant who enjoys a connection with the passer-by, while one with curtains on the window hints that the owners prefer their privacy. Though it is important to be security conscious, this does not need to mean hiding away. What sort of inclusive or exclusive message are we giving through the treatment of our windows?

Think about ways the window can express your personality. If you highlight the window surround, you bring emphasis to the window. Do you want to add window boxes, colour, frivolity and fun? Remember, when you add something to the exterior of the house you are also adding to the street and in turn the village, town or city.

CHECKING OUT THE LIGHT LEVELS

Does your front garden face north, south, east or west? Look at the orientation of your house and consider how natural daylight affects the rooms at the front. The sun rises in the east, bringing with it the early-morning light, which has a warm, orange feel that is naturally invigorating. As the sun rises higher into the sky, we get daylight with a cooler, bluer quality. The sun sets in the west and the light reverts back to warmer, orange hues. Cut back any natural obstructions outside the house that restrict light from entering the

front rooms, including bushes, hedges and trees. A south-facing room will receive all the sunlight and may need to be shaded to prevent it from getting too hot. This can be achieved simply by opening a window at the front and back of the house to create a through-airflow. Other methods include placing shading devices on the exterior of the façade such as awnings, canopies or louvres (see later in chapter). A north-facing room is good to work in as the light is very even and there is no glare from the sun.

If you have a dark room, remember that light bounces and can be reflected into a room from a variety of surfaces. By painting your window frames, sills and surrounds in brilliant white, light will bounce off them and into the room.

If privacy is an issue, or you wish to restrict the amount of sunlight entering the front rooms, try to find ways to obscure vision without blocking out all the natural light. You could obscure the glass (see page 66), fit opaque or textured glass, or use lightweight sheer fabrics as curtains. If it is not necessary to block off the whole window to create privacy, try obscuring just the bottom half. This will allow light to enter the room through the clear glass at the top of the window. A more permanent way of creating the same effect is to use a roller blind mounted on the window sill; with a simple system of pulleys, you can raise the blind to the desired height and tie it off using hooks. Think about how this will look from the outside as well as the inside – it's the outside that people will see first.

Far left: By frosting the glass only in the lower section of the window some privacy is given while a view out is still maintained and light can still enter.

Left: Curtains define the edges of the window. By layering up the thickness of curtains from translucent voile to heavier fabrics you can choose what level of privacy and warmth you want.

DEFINING THE WINDOW

A window will have several fundamental basic elements:
- Glass which permits light to enter and protects the house from the elements
- A frame which pins the window unit to the wall
- A framework which holds the glass
- Hardware which operates and locks the unit.

Windows are either fixed or operable. Where ventilation is a consideration, you will need an operable window. Fixed windows are usually placed where light and views are important but ventilation is not necessary. Most unusually shaped windows are fixed because an opening mechanism might be too complicated. Operable windows move in a variety of ways, from sliding up, down or sideways. Also, depending on the hingeing mechanism, they may open inwards or outwards. Some windows combine fixed and operable glazed areas – this is especially common in windows where glass may be curved on some panes, such as a bay window.

Other important considerations should be how the window defines the interior shape of the room, whether it creates a focal point or even if it provides an emergency escape.

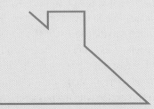

To make more of any available light in your hallway, a good option is to replace a solid door with a glass-panelled one. This allows the light to enter the hall, while retaining a sense of privacy.

REGULATIONS REGARDING RENOVATING, REPLACING OR ADDING WINDOWS

If you are replacing existing windows or creating a new window opening then you need to find out if there are any planning restrictions that will affect your plans. Speak to your local planning officer first. As described in Chapter 2, if your house is listed Grade I, II or II*, then any replacement windows will have to be changed in keeping with the style of the original design of the house. Even if you're not under any obligation to do so, if you think your windows have been changed from the original, you could find out what style of windows your house had initially. Look at the windows on similar buildings on your street for clues, or try to track down an original photograph of your street. If you live in a Conservation Area, you may find that you are restricted to using only one particular type of window for overall uniformity in the street.

NEW BUILDING REGULATIONS

In 2002, new regulations for housing came into force to improve thermal efficiency standards. This has had a big impact on window and door specification, and for the first time, replacement windows to buildings are also covered by the regulations, although there are exemptions permitted for historic buildings.

For new buildings or refurbishment, the minimum glazing specification is a double-glazed window with a hard coat, low-emissivity glass (this reflects the heat out) that has a 16mm air gap and an argon-filled cavity. This is the gap between the glass sheets. If you wish to use this specification you need to prove that the insulation value elsewhere in the house is much greater than the required amount to compensate. Speak to your Building Regulations Officer for more information.

Conservatories

A conservatory is considered separate from the house if there is a wall, window or door dividing it from the rest of the building. These separating elements need to have the same thermal efficiency value as other external elements of the house. In this case no specific values apply to the conservatory. However, if a new opening is made on to a conservatory then the glass of the conservatory is considered as the exterior walls and must satisfy the Building Regulations values.

Ventilation

Building Regulations also require that adequate ventilation is provided, so you must not worsen the room's existing ventilation. All habitable rooms and rooms containing a toilet should have opening windows of at least 1/20th of the floor area of the room. For kitchens, utility rooms and bathrooms, an extractor fan is also normally required.

You cannot block up or remove any permanent vents that were created to supply combustion air to heating appliances. Trickle vents come in plastic or metal, so if you are replacing your window, check if you need to include these ventilation strips. If you are having timber windows made, then make sure the strip is a metal one so that it can be painted in the window colour. In general, these strips are not very attractive, so we recommend fitting them into the wall where possible.

Means of escape

The first-floor windows should be large enough to allow you to escape if you were trapped in the room by a fire. This applies to the ground floor, too, if the room does not open on to a hall with an external door. Windows are required to have an unobstructed openable area of $0.33m^2$ ($1ft^2$) and be not less than 450mm (18in) high and 450mm (18in) wide. You are not required to change your windows if this does not already apply but you are not permitted to worsen your situation if you do change your windows.

NOISE POLLUTION

If you experience a high degree of external noise inside your house from sources such as traffic, aircraft or barking dogs, it is likely that nearly 90 per cent of this noise is coming through the doors and windows. Changing your windows to a high-specification triple-glazing with good acoustic seals is one solution. Alternatively, you could fit soundproof windows behind your existing ones that open and close, so you can still access the exterior windows. Secondary glazing such as this reduces sound pollution by 75–95 per cent, and also reduces drafts and condensation and provides an added layer of security.

TYPES OF WINDOWS

There is a vast array of types and sizes of windows which function differently to serve varying needs. Consider what you want the window to do, then the frame type and then the glazing.

WHAT STYLE OF WINDOW DO YOU HAVE?

There are eight basic types of window found in most homes:

1 **Box sash window.** Includes double-hung (top- and bottom-opening) and single-hung (bottom-opening only), which have a hidden counterweight which enables the window to remain fixed in any open position without sliding down. Traditional sash windows incorporate a lead weight and pulley system, and were glazed using putty pointing (a slimmer appearance and more traditional technique) or timber glazing beads. An alternative method is a spiral balance mechanism. This incorporates a pre-tensioned steel spring and spiral balance, and is often used where the box rebate for the weights is not present. This system allows the option to hinge or tilt the sash for cleaning or as a fire escape.

2 **Slider window.** This is where the window slides to the right or left.

3 **Casement and awning windows.** These swing out from the sides or up or down from the top or bottom. They are available as a flush or storm (overlapping) casements or fanlights.

4 **Fixed panel.** A window that cannot be opened.

5 **Bay window.** The term 'bay' is the same as the general term for any interval between two supports in a building. The main reason for reviving the bay on terraces was the desire for fresh air, especially at the seaside. This was common in traditional architecture and then revived at the beginning of the 19th century.

6 **French window.** Generally a glazed panelled door found most often today at the rear of a property. In Georgian and Victorian terraces, large 'French windows' opened on to verandas or even a small balustrade, giving the appearance of a door to the street. These were mainly on the first-floor level.

7 **Oriel window.** Projecting windows, often circular, that create a cantilever from the façade.

8 **Special architectural forms.** These may be curved or angled.

Left: A top-hung casement window set into a bay of a typical suburban house only opens a little way.

Centre: A sash window, here set into a Victorian house, slides open either from the top or bottom.

Right: The oriel window on the upper level of this suburban house is a quirky feature, and contains stained glass set into the frame.

WINDOW FRAMES

Window frames come in a variety of materials, from timber to UPVC to aluminium or steel. Timber frames are supplied in either softwood or hardwood. Hardwood is recommended for a longer lifespan and if you wish to expose the natural colour of the timber.

Over the last few decades, window companies have used aggressive marketing to try to encourage people to change their windows to double-glazing. All new housing has double-glazing requirements. This has meant that the frames have become thicker and heavier in appearance, which has drastically changed the appearance of houses. Streets are filled with houses where the original windows have been replaced with double-glazed, UPVC-framed windows. Often the replacement windows have no resemblance to the original frame detail, so they look unsightly and incongruous to the original design. It is also not recyclable.

In defence of UPVC, there are obvious benefits – good draft prevention, reduced heat loss, and low maintenance. However, all these aspects are possible from double-glazed windows with a timber frame, with the added advantage that you can choose the colour of your frame. Most timber window companies guarantee the paintwork for up to eight years, so you won't have to repaint for a long period of time. Good joiners can make double-glazed timber frames that are a close duplicate to the original but will have far more slender profiles. It is possible to reproduce Victorian, Edwardian and other frame styles. This is rarely the case with UPVC.

Timber frames have more flexibility in terms of style and they will age with the rest of the materials of your house to give much more character to the property's appearance. This will often add value to your house. You may wish to consider this when deciding whether to spend the extra money on timber frames as opposed to UPVC, which are nearly always less expensive.

Modern slender-framed metal windows are still available, and can look stylish, but you may need to include secondary glazing for insulation. Porthole-shaped windows can also be used for an interesting alternative. In fact, it is now possible to create any shaped window as the glass can be cut to size and shape and fitted into a timber or metal frame, which can be single-, double- or even triple-glazed.

Secondary glazing system

This is an additional frame on the inside face of a window and is a useful way to preserve an original single-glazed window and add insulation to the interior. These are mainly manufactured from slim, unobtrusive white-enamelled aluminium profiles, usually with single-glazing. Double-glazing is also available for specialist applications. These units replicate the design of the main windows and are installed inside them. Alternatively, you can choose minimal framing that has a limited impact on the aesthetic of the exterior window.

THE WINDOW SILL

The profile of the window sill externally acts to dispel water away from the building and internally forms a neat face to hide the wall construction. If you are intending to add some form of cladding to the façade of your house then make sure that your sills will still protrude beyond the face of the house to allow the water to fall away from them.

Traditional sills were also used to hide window shutters. Some of the early sash windows included interior shutters hidden away in a box under a hinged lid, thereby creating a window sill.

MAINTENANCE

Timber windows need to be rubbed down and repainted before the paint completely flakes off the wood. Some old window frames that have woodworm may need replacing in part or in full. It may be possible just to cut out sections of the timber and replace them with either new timber or an epoxy resin, which can be rubbed down and painted to a seamless finish. Always use external oil-based paints and apply a primer first.

Metal windows sometimes corrode. If you can treat them early enough it is possible to rub them down with a wire brush to the bare metal and fill if necessary, and then repaint with an exterior metal paint. Always check with a specialist if you are unsure about the best treatment.

SECURITY ASPECTS AND WINDOW FURNITURE

It is important to ensure you have the window furniture that reflects the style of the window as well as providing the necessary security both for you and your insurance company. Windows need a handle that locks the window shut and sometimes allows the window to lock in a slightly open position for ventilation. Your windows will probably also need an extra lock – there are a variety of these to choose from for every type of window. They include sliding, lockabe window stays that fit along the bottom of the window, fasteners which are lockable handles that sit on the opposite side to the hinges and simple locks that are screwed on the frame. Check what your insurance company requires as any absence can invalidate your insurance.

All these locks can be found in a variety of finishes from painted to brass to steel so shop around for the right style.

The window sill is a handy ledge to display objects of curiosity, a tradition which apparently began when ornamentation was reduced from the façade detail. You could use the objects to say something about your life and liven up the journey of the person who walks past your house daily on their way to work.

GLASS

Glass is a solidified liquid whose molecules have formed in a random order, as opposed to a lattice, giving the glass its transparent quality.

TYPES OF GLASS FOR GLAZING

If you intend to replace existing glass in your home or to create new glazed areas, then you must give some thought to what type of glass will suit the particular application. Glass is not just a simple functional material created to allow light into an area; it can also produce a decorative effect. It is important that the correct type of glass is used so that it is safe, effective and creates the right overall image. The wrong glass can be hazardous and may not meet safety standards.

'Ordinary' sheet glass

This glass is produced using rollers through which the glass is passed. The process creates flat sheets of glass, but the rollers create some distortion on the surface, which can be an irritation. This glass is cheaper than other types and therefore it is often used for glazing greenhouses and other such constructions where its distortion is visually less important.

Float (plate) glass

The name 'float glass' comes from its production technique. The molten glass is 'floated' on to a bed of molten tin. Float glass is flat and free of visual distortions. This glass is also relatively cheap. Float glass can be used for windows above waist height, but not below, as it does not meet Building Regulations. Glass can also be made to be curved or even self-cleaning.

Energy-efficient glass

Known as low-E glass or K glass, this glass is produced by coating one side of float glass with a special thin coating that allows the sun's energy to pass through in one direction and reduces thermal transfer in the other direction. The coating can give a tint to the glass so it appears slightly grey or brown and must be used on the inside of double-glazed units otherwise it will wear off very quickly through weathering and cleaning. Different types of low-E coatings have been designed to allow for high, moderate or low solar gain (the amount of heat you wish to allow through the window from the sun). In addition, for extra thermally insulated glass, the cavity is filled with argon gas.

Obscured, patterned or textured glass

During manufacture, a surface texture is created by rolling the unhardened glass over a roller with a surface imprint, transferring the texture on to the surface of the glass. Textured glass comes as flat sheet glass, and is available in a wide range of patterns, colours and tints. Each glass pattern will give different levels of obscuration to the glass. This level of distortion is usually given a number between one and five; the higher the number, the less you can see any distinct feature through the glass. If you intend to use patterned glass for external glazing, then the patterned side is usually on the inside for ease of cleaning.

Toughened/safety glass

Toughened glass is produced using ordinary float glass. After the glass has been cut to size and prepared, it is heated to approximately 620°C (1148°F), then cooled rapidly. Once treated, it becomes much tougher and more difficult to break. However, if it does break, the glass will shatter into hundreds of small pieces that do not have sharp edges. It is imperative that the treatment takes place after the glass is cut and prepared, as any attempt to cut the glass post-treatment will cause it to shatter immediately. This glass is a good choice for glazed doors, low windows and tabletops.

Coloured glass can add fantastic changing light effects to the inside of your house. Choose from a limited colour palette for a more contemporary effect.

Laminated glass

Laminated glass is made from two or more sheets of glass sandwiched together using a transparent, flexible bonding material. This makes the glass very strong. In the unlikely event of it breaking or cracking, often only one side breaks while the flexible bonding holds the material in place, reducing the likelihood of dangerous sharp edges.

Wired glass

This glass is similar to laminated glass in that sandwiched in the glass is a wire mesh that holds it together, meaning that even if the glass is broken, it is difficult to break through. The spacing of the wire mesh is usually around 10mm (⅜in). The overall look can be quite industrial and can be very unattractive unless you desire this effect. Although the glass holds together if it breaks, it is not considered to be 'safety' glass as it will still break with sharp edges.

Stained glass

Stained glass is a decorative art that has been used in architecture for centuries. It can be made in a variety of forms, designs and colours to any specification. Stained glass is constructed from many pieces of coloured glass that are laid out on a single flat surface, fixed within a frame and held together by lead. Traditionally, the pieces would be 2mm (⅛in) thick. They are cut to size and shape, painted and fired, then arranged into a pattern or design. Stained glass is often found as a detail on doors and windows of houses. Sections of coloured glass can be set straight into openings, frames or doors.

MINI PROJECT Making a stained glass window

Create your own stained glass window by drawing a design on paper, then divide the design into a few defining sections of colour. Cut out each section and fit them back together with a small gap where the lead will be. You will then need to take this design to a stained glass specialist who can make it up. You could also find a contemporary artist who works with stained glass to make a window or panel for your front door.

This etched front door window has had the door number cut out so that light can enter the interior hallway, and small sections are still left visible to see through to the outside.

GLASS SURFACE TREATMENTS

You may wish to change the glass in your windows to create more privacy or give more colour. Coloured glass can cast beautiful light into a room. There are many different methods, some of which involve replacing the glass and are therefore more permanent, while others can be carried out on your existing glass.

Acid etching

This gives glass panels a matt finish that is determined by how long the glass spends in acid. The longer it is dipped, the more the transparency diminishes. By masking areas before dipping, patterns and pictures can be etched into the surface. Most types of glass can be acid-etched.

Sandblasting

This can be used to achieve a matt finish. and creates a similar effect to acid etching but is slightly more textured. Patterns or pictures can be included by masking out particular areas.

Enamelling

During the manufacture of toughened or heat-strengthened glass, enamelling can be done by applying a coloured ceramic layer to the glass surface and baking it. It can be applied in various ways including spraying or silkscreen printing.

Glass paint

This can be applied simply with a brush and forms a strong coating on the glass, which will set hard over a period of around 24 hours. Glass paint can be used to give a stained glass effect.

Spray etch paint

A glass frosting spray-paint can be bought from DIY and craft stores. This can be applied directly on to the window glass, although it could be patchy unless you apply several layers. It is better to use a self-adhesive plastic film that gives a frosted-glass effect, available from most glaziers or DIY stores. A pattern can also be printed into the film. It is best if you get a sign-maker to fit the film on to the glass.

OTHER MATERIALS

For a special effect, or if you need to create a new window to allow more light into the hallway, then you might think of using something unusual.

Glass blocks

These are structural blocks of cast-glass that can be built to be load-bearing. They are generally square-shaped, although they can also be round, and come in a range of colours and textures. The simplest block with a frosted finish gives a clean and contemporary appearance (see Resources, pages 155–157). You will need to use recommended mortar and employ a skilful builder to fit them. Glass 'U' sections are also available in varying lengths with their own system of fixings.

Plastics

Polycarbonates and acrylics can be used as non-shatterproof alternatives to glass, but are difficult to insulate while still maintaining transparency. They also scratch more readily and over time will start to become brittle, so replacing glass windows with polycarbonate is rarely a long-lasting alternative to glass.

OUTSIDE THE WINDOW

The external appearance of your house is largely determined by the windows. Look at the condition of the windows and see whether they enhance the look of your property or lack character and interest.

Decide to what degree applied decoration will benefit the appearance of your house. A particularly ornate window will probably mean that the property already has lots of character and it will be difficult to change or add to this. Most of the properties in *Front of House* had windows with little definition or unique character. The framing of the window, either with a cladding material or simply by painting around the rim, helped to define the house elevation and give importance to these apertures. Look at Jason and Kate's house (see page 52) and the house in the case study on the following page.

Other elements that you can add to the exterior of the house include window boxes, shutters, louvres, awnings and balconies. These will all project out from the façade, giving a more three-dimensional appearance to the house. In the same way that Georgian houses had pediments around the window frames and doors to give proportion and definition, so contemporary features can be added to your own property.

WINDOW BOXES

These are great because not only are you bringing nature close up to the edge of your window, but you are also raising flowers and plants off the ground so that people looking at your house from a distance can enjoy them.

Window boxes require some thought, though, because they need to be attached correctly to the edge of your house and they must be maintained regularly. Ensure the fixing is sufficient for the weight of the earth in the box, especially when filled with water, and make sure that you can open the windows in such a way as to access the plants without damaging them. If access through the windows is not possible, you may be able to run a self-watering system into the pots; the pipe is small and can be fastened subtly to the edge of the window. See Soft Landscaping, pages 134–153, for more suggestions as to suitable and unusual materials, and for ideas for plants to grow.

WINDOW AWNINGS

Traditionally, when light became too bright inside a house, shade was applied through the use of awnings. These were made of lead, though later they came in felt, or fabric, and also often covered the area over a balcony. On the Continent, many houses have fabric awnings, which can be opened over windows at an angle in strong sun. When not in use, these act like a roller blind and fold back against the façade into the casing.

Window awnings can offer an ornamental and colourful addition to any south-facing façade, providing shade to the room inside.

CASE STUDY
Windows for a Princess house

Julie's house had very few features to define it. The windows were incredibly small in relation to the expanse of wall and the door was relatively undefined. Julie disliked the hydrangea plant in front of the house but did have a taste for detail. We decided to try to give this rather bland house a feel somewhere between a country cottage and a palace fit for a princess.

Using reclaimed floor boards for an aged look, thick frames were made around each of the windows with built-in window boxes. Framing the windows this way made them appear larger than they actually are. The frames were then stencilled with butterflies and the window boxes planted with a pink flower to tie into the colour of the butterflies. The flowers were reminiscent of the fairytale of Sleeping Beauty.

The door was framed using wrought ironwork fencing discovered in a salvage yard. These pieces were sanded back and rewelded to make an ornate and elaborate porch that was then painted white. This offered the opportunity for planting to be grown up the trellis at a later date. More floor boards and a feature crown of trellis formed the focus to the porch.

Finally, cut-outs of flying butterflies were also painted pink and applied over the façade. A curvaceous open frame was made for a screen that swept around the front garden to lead up to the entrance (see also page 130). Delicate planting in the front garden complemented the house façade.

SHUTTERS

Generally, timber shutters are a traditional method of covering the windows at night or in very bad weather to protect the glass. They are used mainly on the Continent, where it is common to have open painted timber or metal shutters on either side of the window as part of the picturesque image of the house. Often the difficulty with these is getting access to them on the upper levels. Normally, these windows would open inwards. Shutters can also be bought as a decorative element.

BALCONIES

To add a balcony is not a small job, but if you have always wanted one then consult an architect to advise. You may need planning permission, and if you are the only house in the street to have one then it is unlikely you will get it. If, however, you live in an area with an eclectic mix of property and the balcony is in keeping with your own house, then you stand more chance. You will need to support the balcony structurally and so advice from an engineer will be necessary. There are also a number of manufacturers that can advise you. Note that the height of a balustrade for Building Regulations requirements is 1100m (43in).

SECURITY GRILLES

If you feel anxious about crime, and feel it is necessary to have grilles fitted to your windows, then there are a number of standard metal grille options available to you. However, grilles can also be made to feature ornate designs, leaves and flowers or contemporary twists and patterns to enhance your home. Get a metalwork company to weld your own pattern or go to an artist for help with ideas. Some grilles retract so that you only shut them when you go away on holiday or at night.

PLASTER SURROUNDS

Window surrounds can be added in fibreglass, expanded foam or plaster moulds of traditional features such as pilasters, ornate sills, corbels or heads to windows. These will imitate those originally produced in stone, but are usually made from stucco or plaster. Ornamentation copied from history was usually connected with a sense of status and wealth. To subvert this meaning, why not try adding a few extra details and painting them out of context like in the eccentric England with a Twist house (see page 20). Do some research to find the best company to reproduce these items for you.

This window grille has been given a symmetrical, organic design so the grille is not perceived as window bars but rather as a design for the framing of the window, which works well with the urn placed centrally on the sill beyond.

CASE STUDY
Diamond house shutters

The couple that lived in this house wanted a Mediterranean house and garden. Unfortunately, the original dark brickwork did not lend itself to a ready transformation to the light-coloured houses seen on the Continent. The first thing that had to be done was to render the front façade and the side wall so that the house appeared brighter and lighter.

A typical feature of European windows was used to frame the windows. Shutters were added to either side to provide a focus and give definition. On the Continent shutters are used on windows both as shading devices from the sun and to keep out the extremes of cold weather and gales. For this house the shutters were purely for decoration.

Horizontal banding was added to the walls to break up the proportions of the house and a criss-cross arrangement of red rope was then fixed to the exterior as an alternative version of the timber framing that is common on this type of house in Europe.

A large canopy was intended to be hung from one side of the house to form a covered garden seating area typical of an Italian domestic garden, so that the inhabitants could eat outdoors if the weather permitted. However the time pressures of filming for television meant that this became a smaller, more discreet, canopy, although one still suitable for dining 'al fresco'.

INSIDE THE WINDOW

Equally important and seen from both the outside and inside is the treatment that you give to your windows internally.

WINDOW COVERINGS

When you think of domestic window coverings, the first thing that often springs to mind is net curtains. This is a traditional treatment that, although it suits many situations, is not the only thing on offer. There is a wide variety of window coverings on the market. You may even discover you cannot find exactly what you are looking for – this can easily be resolved as there are many specialists who will make up bespoke window coverings to specification, although this can become expensive. Why not rethink your idea for something new or make it yourself? Window coverings are quite simple to produce and, with a little effort, some great effects can be achieved.

Firstly, you need to decide on the structural style that would suit your home. Remember that your window coverings make an impact on both the interior and exterior of your home. Think about coordination throughout the house – a house viewed from the outside with many different types of window coverings can look very patchy. It is possible to have different patterns on the inside and out so that the curtains internally match the room and externally are consistent to match the exterior of the house.

It is important to consider the overall style of the architecture of your house before making a decision. Although modern blinds look great, they may not suit all houses, just as ornate, voluptuous drapes may look ridiculous on small modern houses.

Curtains

If you prefer to choose curtains for your home, there are many styles and fabrics that you can select from with which to create an individual look. Fabric offers enormous scope for creating window coverings.

Ready-made curtains are available in a variety of lengths and widths to fit many window sizes and are available with all types of fixings. They are usually unlined and quite lightweight. Alternatively, custom-made draperies are usually lined, possibly pleated and custom-produced to fit the exact dimensions of your window opening. Curtains are traditionally hung via the rod and rings method. Draperies can be hung on traverse rods, which allow the panels to be opened or closed with a hidden cord.

Types of exotic fabrics include linens and silks, which can be subtle and beautiful to view, though the colour can fade over time in direct sunlight. Your choice of window covering may also act as a drauht barrier, keeping warmth inside your home – heavier fabrics such as velvets and wools are best. Consider making curtains from a blanket on wire cables as an alternative approach.

Blinds

There are various styles of blinds available that vary according to their opening mechanism. The main styles of blinds in use these days are roller blinds, Roman blinds and Venetian blinds. Although other styles do exist – festoon or Austrian, for example – they are generally considered out-dated.

Until their recent use in contemporary design, roller blinds were usually only found in kitchens and bathrooms. This type often suits contemporary design as it is simple in appearance and function.

To add some individuality to your fabric pattern you could design your own print. Printing a fabric can be a simple process and there are many products on the market with which to produce your own designs. Check to see how they can be applied and how the fabric should be washed. Effects can be created very simply by using an object as a stamp; the top of a jar, for instance, will produce a circular design which can be used to create a geometric pattern or something more flamboyant. Use your imagination, look around for objects in interesting shapes and think about the designs you can achieve.

You could also have your own designs/photographs printed directly on to fabric. If you have a photographic manipulation computer program such as Photoshop, you could create a fantastic JPEG image which you could have printed

directly on to fabric. There are various companies that offer this service including sign-makers, specialist printers and exhibition stand specialists.

Another simple way of customizing your own curtains/blinds is to stitch on additional features (as above).

Today, Roman blinds are the most popular alternative to curtains. Roman blinds fold on to themselves in a concertina action. These blinds can be created with a hard, defined or soft look, depending on the fabric used and the method of construction. For a harder look, horizontal bars would be added at each fold.

Venetian blinds come in both horizontal and vertical designs. These are very good if you are particularly concerned with light control, as it is easy to regulate the amount of light entering your house using these blinds. One thing to bear in mind is how synonymous these window coverings have become with office buildings. Do you want this look in your home?

These blinds can work well with very large expanses of glazed areas that are usually only found on very modern buildings.

Blinds can be made up in almost any fabric provided the density of the fabric does not hinder the working mechanism. Some companies offer a laminating service which can stiffen virtually any soft furnishing fabric and prepare it for use as a blind (while retaining the initial surface texture of the chosen fabric). This service is particularly handy if wish to coordinate your window coverings with the other fabrics around your room.

One great advantage of choosing blinds as your window coverings is that when they are raised they take up very little space, so maintaining visibility to most of the glazed area and allowing maximum light to enter the building when you want it to.

Blinds can be created to be adaptable to most contours including domes or angled roofs. Various fabrics can be used, including technical fabrics, which provide protection against heat gain and ultra-violet rays.

VISIBILITY

Take care when choosing a fabric for your curtains/blinds. Your choice will not only have an effect on the overall appearance and décor, but will also affect the amount of visibility and light that passes through the coverings. Fabrics vary an enormous amount in their levels of transparency – when choosing them, bear in mind the amount of privacy you require. If you have a sheer fabric, even if it blocks visibility throughout the day you will find that when it is dark outside and lights are on inside your house, you may be on display to the rest of the street!

For a bedroom, depending on your preferred light conditions for sleeping, you may want to use blackout fabric (this can be used on curtains or blinds). This fabric prevents any light from passing through it. It is usually sold as a liner for curtains or as ready-made blinds, but it can be laminated on to almost any fabric by a blind-maker.

If you do use linings on your curtains, you should remember that this will have an effect on the exterior look as the curtains will have a different appearance on each side.

OTHER WINDOW COVERINGS

Materials that can be used as window coverings do not stop at fabrics. There are many other materials that could be used. Japanese design is noted for its use of paper screening, which creates a stunning effect. Many of these traditional Japanese materials are permeable in nature, which means they disperse light. The screens act as porous walls, which disperse and filter light rather than block it; this acts as a subtle tool for visual privacy.

MECHANISMS

Motorized window treatments are now widely available. Operation of the systems can be by wall switch or remote control. Electronic controls can easily be integrated into a home. Automatic curtain-closing can be convenient from many points of view; as well as the ease-of-use aspect, it gives the impression that the home is always inhabited, which is a good security feature.

Finally, instead of the traditional nets, there are a wide range of voile fabrics that can be draped down in front of your window to add a subtle amount of screening between you and the outside.

The house for Larna has been fitted with horizontal metal Venetian blinds. These were chosen for this house to coordinate with the other industrial-looking materials that are used on the outside of the building. The blinds give a modernist look, providing clean, strong lines and substantial materials.

CASE STUDY
Claire's fruit machine blinds

This house already had a good deal of character, featuring a projecting glass porch with windows made up of four identical panes. The dormer windows popping up through the roof already appeared as miniature beach huts looking out to sea. To continue this theme, each dormer was painted a seaside colour. Semi-transparent fabric was chosen from a sign-maker and four large scaled-up images of the typical symbols found in fruit machines, such as cherries and bells, were printed on to the fabric. Each piece of fabric was carefully measured to cover each of the four panes of glass. They were then made up into roller blinds, which could be lowered over the entire window to display the symbols. The blinds could be used for privacy or to shade the large amount of glazing from sunlight, whilst filtering light into the house and carrying the

sense of fun portrayed in the seaside concept through on to the exterior. A game could be played by pulling the blinds up or down to reveal different fruit machine icons.

In addition, cladding was added below these windows in a similar style to the tiling found on the roofs of piers in a seaside town. The cladding was coloured silver to reflect the light and glisten like fish scales.

The door number was designed to bring to mind funfair lighting (see page 49) and the flags added movement, colour and a sense of arrival.

The front garden was created with added playful features like a see-saw and a sandpit for the children in the shape of an ice-cream cone (see page 120). The owners, especially the children, were very excited by their new seaside house.

DOS AND DON'TS

DO

- Get your windows cleaned regularly, it will make a real difference to the amount of light coming through them.
- Remove any obstructions that may block light from your window, such as greenery or foliage.
- Repaint wooden frames every few years to keep them from rotting.
- Paint window frames and sills white to help bounce light into the interior.
- Think about how your curtains look from the outside when they are drawn. Keep them clean and line them with a fabric to co ordinate with the façade of your house.
- Fit window locks now!

DON'T

- Fit windows to your house that don't suit the architecture, such as leaded light PVC frames on a Victorian house.
- Obscure the passage of light into the interior with thick curtains that don't fully open. Use voiles to obscure views in the house for daytime use.
- Put prison-like bars over your window – consider more decorative security solutions for your home.

CHAPTER 5
WALLS AND BOUNDARIES

What we do to our walls is important to us, which isn't surprising as they constitute most of the front of our homes. In the making of *Front of House* one phrase was repeated over and over again as anxious homeowners were whisked away: 'Don't clad our house in fake stone or paint it pink!' But they didn't need to worry as there are many other options open to us when considering the design and decoration of our walls. What may at first seem to be a limited palette can soon become a blank canvas if you know what the options are. We used a variety of paints, cladding materials and decorative finishes to bring the walls of Britain alive. Many of these were used in conjunction with one another, creating exciting results.

WHAT TO DO TO YOUR WALLS

Between the windows and doors lies the remaining ingredient that constitutes the external appearance of the house – the walls. The chosen finish we give to this surface will become the face of our streets.

A façade of Georgian terrace houses has been brightened up by painting each one a strong colour, giving an individual identity to each house but a feeling of uniformity to the whole.

We can choose to expose the structural material of the wall such as a brick façade or cover it over with paint or cladding (cladding is the term used to describe any type of material, such as metal or glass, used to cover the surface of another). Cladding has been used to decorate the façades of buildings for hundreds of years. When it became too expensive to use a structural material that could be exposed, an alternative was to make an imitation of the intended finish and add this to a cheaper structural material. An example of this was in the Georgian period: when stone was too expensive, stucco (a type of plaster render) was used over the brickwork and given indented lines to appear as slabs of stone.

Just as we adorn ourselves by getting dressed up or wearing jewellery to add beauty, colour and interest, so there are many methods to layer the façade to really make a difference to the appearance of your house. So much of our environment lacks a sense of personality. Whether you are looking to make a bold change or add some colour to brighten up a rather dreary, tired-looking front wall, there are many ways to go about it. It is about time we brought back life, individuality and creativity to our streets.

Before making any decisions on personalizing your house you should first consult with your local council. They will be able to tell you if there are any regulations governing what you can and cannot do in that area. Different areas have different regulations so there are no fixed rules on this.

Once you have found out whether restrictions apply, you can come up with a scheme. See Chapter 2, 'Getting Started', (pages 23–35) for advice on how to begin. Even if restrictions do apply to your home, it is still possible to make changes but within a more limited arena. Look at your façade as a canvas on which to begin a work of art. There are many modern and old materials that could be used in different ways from those for which they were intended. These could create stunning effects, so be creative.

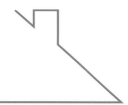

PERMITTED CHANGES
If your house is not listed and is not in a Conservation Area, then changes that are considered 'temporary' should be allowed.

ADDING A SPLASH OF COLOUR

Paint is one of the easiest and cheapest ways to freshen up the façades of your house.

This Tudor house shows an example of the typical florid style of painting that would have been used to decorate the houses of the period.

Once your walls have been made good and prepared it is also one of the first operations that will need to take place. Paint offers an opportunity to make a real impact, making the property look cleaner, tidier and more respectable and even adding personality to your home. It can form the scheme in its own right or complement other design elements of your property.

There are many ways paint can be used on façades. Most people have seen whole houses painted in various colours. Often this is a single colour with a highlight colour used for features, such as windows and door surrounds. There is also the idea of applying colour as a mural. There are many examples of this, from the earliest painters adding floral designs onto houses, to artists painting large and detailed murals, to graffiti artists who use walls for self-expression or social comment. The messages are mixed, some seen as a social contribution to the environment – enlivening a dull area, and giving 'life' to a building – while other works are seen as disrespectful, a nuisance and even threatening. What can be said is that by painting an individual scheme on to a wall, you are expressing yourself in the public domain.

SELF-EXPRESSION IN PAINTING

When deciding to paint your house it is worth considering that your home is part of a larger community, affected by other people and nature. This picture is never static but changes with the time of day, the movement of people, the changes of neighbouring buildings and the growth of plants. See 'Getting Started' (pages 23–35) for a look at how to choose your colours and decide on colour schemes.

Town planning legislation has taken away some of the freedom of the individual for free design and it is always worth remembering to check first with local planners on any restrictions or listings. The colour you choose to paint the front may be a given attribute to your house or your area.

Remember that you are not working with an entirely blank canvas – there are always colours of the roof, ground and other claddings to consider in relation to your colour scheme. Within a rural location it may be relevant to consider the colour of local stone, which gives an area its character.

In a highly polluted area, it may be helpful to paint your house a darker general colour and contrast this with a light colour on the doors and window surrounds. This contrast will make the house look cleaner for longer.

If you live in a semi-detached or terraced house it may be courteous to discuss paint colours with your neighbours. This could be a real bone of contention, particularly if your neighbour feels that your colour scheme may affect the value of their property, and they were not consulted. If you're lucky, they may even want to paint their house the same colour, and split the cost of the paint.

HOW TO PREPARE THE SURFACE

A common problem with painted houses is the paint flaking off. This must be removed prior to re-painting otherwise the new coat of paint will also not adhere. Remove old paint using a wire brush or sandpaper, rubbing down until you get to a stable surface. If you are painting over layers of paint without removing them completely, then it is advisable to give the paintwork a coat of stabilizing solution beforehand. Stabilizing solution acts as a bonding substance between the underlying layers of paint and is similar to primer, stopping the surface being so absorbent, so less paint is required. You may also want to treat the façades with a fungicidal wash to remove mould and algae before painting.

TYPICAL COLOURS FOUND IN AREAS OF THE UK

Region	Colour and Cladding
Eastern counties of England and Scotland	Painted rendering or plastered walls with door and windows picked out, often in white or grey
Suffolk	Pink
Fife	Pale buffs and yellows
Essex and Hertfordshire	Weatherboard cladding painted black with windows and doors in white
Kent	Weatherboard cladding painted white
Kent and Essex	Muted pink as original render was mixed with bull's blood
Yorkshire and further north	Colour less common leaving houses as their stone finish
Western counties of England, Wales and Scotland	Black and white paint
Cheshire	Tudor-style black and white half-timbered houses originated here
Lowlands	Most adventurous use of colour

TYPES OF PAINT

The choice of paint types is often as baffling as the choice of colours, so here is a brief summary of each. In general, a matt finish paint is used for walls and a gloss or semi-gloss for features, windows and doors. It is harder to get a good finish with a gloss paint, but it is easier to clean. Don't compromise on the quality of the paint as this will reduce its life expectancy. In principle, paints with a greater quantity of pigment and binder will be of better quality. For a long-lasting finish it is advisable always to use a primer first and then either an undercoat or just a top coat of colour depending on the manufacturer's recommendations.

Most paint currently on sale contains solvents and VOCs (volatile organic compounds). These can be an irritant to the skin and harmful to the environment. It is possible to buy environmental paint that does not contain harmful products. For many years, lead was used in paint, which caused a range of health effects but lead paint is now banned in the UK. See 'Resources', pages 155–157 for some suppliers.

Exterior emulsion paints

These are suitable for masonry and wood surfaces. High-performance acrylic multi-surface paints are suitable for unpainted wood and even metal, if it has been properly prepared. Exterior emulsions are usually water-based. They come in matt and satin finishes which give protection and colour, are quick drying, have a low odour and tend to be environmentally friendly. They allow surface to breathe, minimizing blistering and flaking caused by moisture and come in one or two coat systems, using primer/top coats.

Masonry paints

These can be used on walls of masonry, render, pebbledash, concrete and brick. They come in smooth or textured finishes and are available as one-coat products. These are fine-textured, resin-based paints with an oil base that come in strong, bright colours. They often contain fungicide for anti-mould properties. Smooth finishes resist dirt while the textured finishes hide minor blemishes.

Cement paints

These are essentially a thick plaster coating. Recent advances have made coloured cements a natural alternative to resin-based paints. They have been re-introduced in a range of earth-based colours for rendering and mortars.

Gloss paints

These are oil-based paints used for exterior woodwork and some metals. They come in satin and gloss finishes and provide a tough and durable protective coat. They are often made up with solvents that provide a hard, smooth finish but tend to crack over time. They are not as environmentally friendly as water-based paints, are slower to dry and give off more odour.

Primers

These provide bonding (helping the top coat stick to the surface) and stain blocking (preventing stains from bleeding through). If priming metal, look for anti-corrosion and anti-rust properties; for wood, check on the can for stain blocking properties; for walls look for a 'primer sealer'.

Specialist paints

Also available is metal paint for railings, drain-pipes, garage doors and fencing; waterproof paint made of bitumen for metal gutters, drain-pipes and concrete; and decorative effect paint for earthenware and ornamentation. Check with each manufacturer's guidelines before applying any paint for specific instructions.

PAINT STYLES AND EFFECTS

Trompe l'oeil

This is an effect that creates an illusion, usually of a three-dimensional object that is not there and is a common feature of Mediterranean buildings. In Paris in recent years there has been a revival of artists painting super-realist murals, portraying things like a window on to a blank area of wall that looks identical to a real window, with curtains, shadows and even a person looking out.

Stencils

Have you ever thought about using decoration in a similar way on the interior and exterior of your home? If you wish to add a graphic to your building, stencils can be a very useful tool, and are available in a huge array of designs. Stencils can add detail that will complement and accentuate your design (as seen in the Japanese house, page 82, where a cherry blossom stencil was used). Some stencil companies will enlarge the size of an image if requested, allowing you to make the motif more visible on the exterior. You could always create your own stencil by cutting out a template from thick card.

The main thing to bear in mind is the suitability of your surface. To achieve highly defined results, then the smoother the surface the better. If you have a stippled surface it will be very difficult to get clear outlines, so consider rendering over the surface to make it smooth.

Projections

Another simple possibility for creating a graphic on your walls is to create an image and then, using a projector (either a video, or a slide/overhead projector), to project the image on to the wall. This gives you the freedom to do something that may not be possible using

Stencils have been added in a band across Elaine's house. The stencils in blue on a fresh white background give the house a Mediterranean feel, which is furthered by the addition of planters. The house number has also been projected onto the house, adding interest to an otherwise plain section of wall and making the most of the house number.

a stencil, such as creating super-size text or numbers, decorative flourishes or shadow outlines of plants, flowers or even animals. The possibilities are endless, allowing you to create something totally unique, to scale and with a level of detail that would not otherwise be possible. Projections are a great way of putting complicated images onto wall surfaces.

Projections are ideally done at dusk or at night-time to allow the light to show up most visibly on the wall; they should then be drawn around in a pencil outline. These lines can be painted in during the day when the paint is likely to dry more easily.

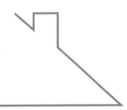

Don't paint on windy days – dust and dirt will get blown around and will stick on to your freshly painted surface. Always check the weather forecast before starting to paint. If rain is imminent, then hold off; it can make water-based paints wash away and gloss paints lose their shine.

CASE STUDY
A Japanese-style house

This original post-war house was made of dark brown brick that provided no definition to the unusual arrangement of windows. The windows added interest but were overshadowed by the heavy and monotonous brickwork.

Julie wanted an oriental-style design so the house was clad in a series of rectangular horizontal panels that had been painted in tonal shades to suggest a sense of oriental geometry and made sense of the unusual window pattern. The colours for the house were all chosen from a palette of browns, and created a tonal colour scheme that is both calming and visually pleasant. The colours are graduated in bands of different shades from light to dark, and were inspired by from the tonal shades found in the brick work. An accent colour of cherry blossom pink was applied using a stencil to give a delicate feminine edge to the design. The overall effect still felt in character with the property.

An additional series of frosted acrylic panels were added to the ground floor wall, creating a soft translucent backdrop for the bamboo that Lisa planted. These panels were then backlit by a net light, creating a soft intriguing glow.

Finally, a Japanese style pergola was added to the front entrance to give a further three-dimensionality to the house. This was created using thick timbers fixed together to leave a small shadowed gap between each join. This idea took inspiration from a typical Japanese building technique which turns the simple details into defining features.

Brick can often be a tricky material to transform but by cladding just a small section of it, an oriental style was created that added colour and visual delicacy and gave a new sense of composition to this otherwise heavy masculine piece of architecture.

CLADDING

What is the underlying fabric of your house? Do you have an existing form of cladding on your house? Any material that covers the main structure of a building is known as a cladding.

This is an example of a decorative technique called pargetting and is a great way to clad walls and add ornamentation.

Cladding is an external, often lightweight, covering or skin applied to a structure. It is important to know what job you need the cladding to do before deciding on the material – whether it is for aesthetic or protective purposes, or both. While some claddings go in and out of fashion – stone cladding or pebbledashing – timber seems to last the test of time.

REMOVING CLADDING

If you want to remove cladding, there may be other work you will have to undertake in order to maintain the building's weatherproofing and protection from damp. If you remove a render, stone or pebbledash clad then you will almost certainly need to re-point the brickwork of your house. To add further protection, a silicon coat can be added to the brick (which should not be applied before six weeks after re-pointing to give the pointing a chance to dry). The silicon coat can be purchased in DIY stores and is simple to paint on. This prevents moisture from entering the surface of the house.

It is important to distinguish between what is a waterproof layer and what is a decorative layer – if your house is a timber-framed building, all that is protecting your house between the timber frame and the outside is the cladding. In these situations, seek professional advice before removing or adding anything.

Removing cladding can be quite a laborious job. If the house is rendered, you will have to slowly chisel off the old render in order not to damage the underlying brickwork. Timber cladding is fixed with screws or nails, so ensure all the old fixings have been removed before applying the new finish.

WHEN TO USE CLADDING

Cladding is used for different reasons, from disguising an element of a house to adding decoration. Originally, rough planks were used to cover timber-frame houses to protect them from the elements. Slates, bricks, clay tiles and rendering were also used to give protection.

Cladding types can be combined and hung off the wall in various directions, shapes and sizes. Think about the composition of the house and your neighbours. What happens at the junctions, the sides of the house and the edges of the windows? It is the details such as these that are important to think through before starting, as it could be costly to deal with them later.

New cladding materials are continually being developed. Before deciding to use a new material or a material that is not usually used as cladding, do some general research. Check on its expected longevity, how it should be maintained, how it is to be fixed to the façade and whether it will be affected by direct sunlight.

CASE STUDY
Mondrian cladding

An example of an innovative use of cladding can be seen in the design of Barry and Kerry's house. The odd shape of the building presented a real challenge – it required a design which took advantage of the unusual asymmetric form of the building. Taking a style of art found in the 1920's and inspired by the artist Piet Mondrian, as a starting point, the house was divided into a series of vertical and horizontal bands and sections. The house was initially painted white to create a blank canvas, then lengths of dark stained lacquered wood were added to divide the house into sections and give it a sense of geometric form. Vibrantly coloured acrylic plastic rectangular blocks were attached to the timbers to set off the scheme. By attaching the plastic to the lengths of wood, the colour panels stood in slight relief to the building.

Acrylic is an interesting material as it is coloured and translucent, allowing light to pass through it whilst still casting shadows on the face of the house. This allows a transformation that occurs throughout the day as the light from the sun moves across the façade of the house. The whole effect is one of vibrancy, colour and a geometric, but asymmetrical, composition.

TIMBER CLADDING

The UK was once covered almost entirely with dense forests which is why, for centuries, timber was used for house construction. Although these have diminished considerably, the UK still has much indigenous timber, such as birch, poplar, rowan, willow and fir, originally from the north of Britain, and oak, elm, hazel, ash, alder, lime, beech and hornbeam from the south. The Romans brought across chestnut, walnut and fruit trees and as the world was explored further, so tropical plants were imported. As well as using resources from the mainland, the UK also imports cut timber.

Green issues

Timber used in cladding should be from sustainable, durable species and from certified suppliers. An advantage of cladding exposed elevations is that external insulation can be incorporated behind the cladding. A further environmental option is to use natural-breathing finishes on the cladding and avoid clear finishes that lack UV protection.

Seasoning the timber

Before use, wood has to be dried out and sap removed to make it stable: until it is fully dried it will be in a process of contraction, which means it may warp or crack. The best timber to use is oak, which, if cared for, has an indefinite life. English oak, however, is difficult to season and is therefore often used 'green', meaning that it is not dried. Green wood still has considerable potential for movement, but this is allowed for by building methods.

Styles of timber cladding

Timber cladding can be used in many ways. It can be cut to simulate stone or brickwork, or into a type of fish-scale pattern tile to clad the upper half of a house with traditional horizontal cladding on the lower half. After World War II, weatherboarding became very fashionable and it was used not only horizontally, but vertically, in the Scandinavian style.

Using timber-board

Timber can also be used as a surface on to which paint or another finish can be applied. Sheet timber needs to be waterproof ply or waterproof (preferably formaldehyde-free) mdf which, once treated, must be sealed with exterior lacquer on the face, back and edges. Different shapes can be cut out and added to your house to add relief. For example, butterfly shapes were cut out for Julie's house façade (see page 68).

Another example of the use of boards can be seen in the colourful and complex painted façade of Chris's house (see page 20). The boards were carefully cut to size and painted before they had been hung so that a precise straight edge to each colour could be achieved more easily and so that they could be sealed before invisibly fixing them to the house. All fixings must be of galvanized or stainless steel or other non-rusting materials of the required strength to support the wood.

Timber imitations and PVCu cladding

Products also exist that look like wood but do not require the same maintenance. A weatherboard effect can be achieved using PVCu cladding strips. Alternatively, there is a range called 'Weatherboarding' (see 'Resources', pages 155–157), which is a cement-based product which can be cut and fixed like timber and painted any colour but will not deteriorate like wood. However, the disadvantage of this is that the building will not weather and take on the aged appearance that gives it character.

CASE STUDY
Timber cladding for a Leafy house

Tracy's house is a large semi-detached brick building with a high brick side-wall and a high pitched roof. The amount of red brick is overpowering. Using the fancy woven-style brickwork on the side wall as inspiration, the design uses the weaving as a basis to break up the heaviness of the brick. Batons and dowels were attached to the house and side wall, and thin strips of plywood were cut and woven in and out of the dowel to create a screen-like structure. The edges of the building were also picked out in this manner. The wood was stained so it was a similar colour to the brickwork. As a continuation of the screening of the brick, the corner section of the building was clad with large cut-out leaves and flowers. The flowers were cut out of wood and attached in slight relief to the building; they

are painted in a red hue which was picked out from the brighter elements of the brickwork. The subtle differences in texture and colour break down the harsh impact of the brick without making the individual elements scream out from the building.

Finding a balance with brick houses can be difficult. Too much brick can be heavy and monotonous, but cladding or painting the whole façade can be costly and time consuming. So find a way of taking the eye away from the brick by adding visual texture and detail, much as one would for an interior by using decorative items such as wall paper. Use colours from the same tonal range as the brickwork to reduce the visual impact of the texture and to give a harmonious feel to the design.

Right: This 'Straw Bale' house was an innovative design that used alternative materials in unusual ways. The straw acts as the structure and provides insulation and is protected from the weather by corrugated clear plastic sheeting.

Far right: On Mark and Louise's house, the 60s 'crazy paving' style stone cladding was replaced by a natural slate stone cladding, which comes in small pieces like mosaic. The new stone provides a uniform colour and flush finish, giving it a contemporary appearance alongside the new timber front door.

MUD

In recent years there has been a revival of cladding and wall construction using old-fashioned and environmentally friendly techniques. It can be used for new walls and so is worth considering for extensions, front walls or even porches. Mud is a cheap, widely available natural resource that is cool in summer and warm in winter.

One system for creating mud structures is using clay bats, which are solid compressed blocks made from a mixture of yellow clay and straw with a rammed dry earth walling. Alternatively, a cob wall can be constructed from local earth, fine sand and gravel, together with a small percentage of imported clay, bound with straw. Mud walls need to sit on a stone or brick plinth and have good overhanging protective capping at the top. Straw is a good element in this mixture as it provides fibrous structural integrity to the mix, and acts as a good insulator due to the air pockets within its structure.

STONE

Stone was used originally as a building material due it's fire-resistance. Some of the earliest stone houses would have been built complete with stone beds and stone cupboards. Many houses will have been constructed using a local stone inherent to the region and there are examples of this throughout the UK. Nowadays, stone is rarely used to construct complete houses due to

its high cost, so instead we see it used more as a cladding material.

Within the UK there is a huge variety of stone available in all types, colours and degrees of strength. Igneous rocks like granite are some of the hardest and most durable. Sedimentary rocks such as sandstone and limestone are softer. In coastal regions especially, flint has a long history of being used for building. It is irregular in shape and often rounded off by the sea. Flint is found within chalk deposits, usually in areas without other good natural stone resources. One great advantage of flint is that it is easy to transport, so it has proliferated outside its regional source areas. Flint was often used in conjunction with other materials as a decorative feature, perhaps in a chequer-pattern. It can be seen used as a cladding on the face of the house, either roughly cut or as smooth pebbles. The rough face of flint makes a beautiful reflective surface which, when used over a large expanse, can produce a stunning effect.

Metamorphic rocks are those that have changed their state, such as slate or marble. They are tough stones and are often used as a building material for roads and roof tiles. Slate can also be used as a cladding material either as a flat finish or overlapping tile.

Consult a good builder or stone manufacturer for details on how to fix the stone. There are specialist suppliers and installers of stone fixings for cladding. If you are mounting the stone directly on to the structure of the house, ensure that the existing wall will support the additional weight of the stone. If in doubt, consult a structural engineer. Stone used as a rainscreen cladding needs to be grouted in the joints, whereas if used as a decorative finish it can be left as open joints. This is a modern way to use cladding and yet it still expresses the honesty of the material. Check whether you need to make provision for movement joints (this is a small flexible joint that prevents the cladding from cracking should movement occur).

BRICKS

Bricks are still probably the most common material to find on the front of houses, having been used as a building material for hundreds of years. The advantage of using brick is its regular shape and durability. Bricks offer fire resistance, they weather well and are easy to use. The dimensions of the first bricks were made to fit a hand for ease of laying, which probably explains why they became so popular.

This Jacobethan bay window shows an interesting use of brickwork. The bricks have been set in a herringbone arrangement as a feature to the side elevation of the house.

The raw material of clay is in plentiful supply in the UK. The huge variety of colours and types of bricks on offer depend on the minerals present in the earth, the method of firing or the additives, such as sand, used in the mixture.

Bricks have undergone transformations over the years, going in and out of fashion. The earliest bricks, called Flemish bricks, were hand-made and were smaller and irregular in size. Nowadays we have the production means to manufacture precisely sized brick made from only cement and sand lime with no clay, which are available in their natural greyish-white or with pigment added. These are often used in low-cost housing and also where the form or shape of a house is to be expressed rather than the surface texture or decoration. Often, poor-quality brickwork is covered over with stucco or render.

Laying bricks

Once you have your bricks, you may wish to consider how to lay them. Typical brick bonding is known as a 'stretcher bond'. This consists of laying the bricks with all their sides showing and is practical for the type of construction most commonly carried out – the cavity wall. This is made up of two skins, the outer in a single-brick thickness and the inner typically consisting of block-work wall. Historically, a number of other bonds were used, including the 'header bond', in which all the ends of the bricks were shown; the 'English bond' consisting of alternate lines of bricks laid end and sideways on; and the weaker, more decorative, 'Flemish bond' bricks laid end on and sideways alternatively in the same course.

Depending on how a bricklayer sets out the bricks, a number of patterns can be achieved, from variegated to herringbone. Traditionally, combining colours of bricks has often been used to achieve further decorative effect.

BRICK TYPES All these bricks are supplied at single stockists and can be laid in interesting patterns or techniques for garden walls, porches or new extensions.

Colour of Brick	Local to	Mineral present
Red	Lancashire	Iron
Blue	Lancashire	Burnt at high temperatures
Brown	Humberside	Lime and little iron
Yellow	Thames Valley	Some chalk or sulphur
White	Sussex and East Anglia	Lime but no iron
Grey	Oxfordshire	Lime but no iron
Black	Oxfordshire	Magnesium

TILES

The use of tiles in architecture has been governed by both their decorative and practical appeal. Tiles are long-lasting and are easy to clean, and so will maintain their original look. Tiles can also be added or removed without affecting the structure of a building. This is where they differ from other architectural ceramics, such as glazed bricks, which become an integral part of the building.

Apart from major tile manufacturers, there are a number of artists and crafts-people who produce handmade tiles of an astonishing variety and who can produce bespoke designs to your own specification. There is also a trade in reclaimed tiles if you would like to use more traditional tiles.

Mosaic tiles can also be used, inside the porch for example. Details around the front door of the house are often more important than the overall look of the house as this is where you will have most contact with the exterior of the house.

Left: Mosaic can be wonderful, but it will be a labour of love, so complete a small section first before taking on the whole house.

Right: Lolly's house had exposed corner brickwork. To tie in with this, green glazed tiles were applied in lines across the top of the house, interspersed with darker green painted sections. The aim was to offset the heavy bricks and add a sense of fun with nature-inspired colours.

It is worth remembering that cladding goes in and out of fashion. When this bungalow was built it was given a coating of pebbledash, a material that is now thought to be drab and very out of date.

RENDERING

Rendering, or plastering, has been used as a method of waterproofing and draught-proofing since primitive construction systems. It is also used to give a uniform effect over the entire surface of a building, rather than the varying surface textures of individual stones or bricks. At the end of the 19th century, pebbledashing became popular as a means to conceal imperfections on the building simply and economically, and disguise the dull colour of render that was available. The technique involved throwing pebbles on to the surface of the render whilst still wet.

If you are rendering a large area of the façade, you may need to allow for expansion joints to ensure no cracking occurs. A good builder should take this into consideration.

Cementitious board is a far less messy alternative to using rendering but provides the same effect. Boards are fixed to the house on to a frame and the gaps filled with external filler and then sanded back to give an even finish. This is a difficult job and should not be attempted unless you have experience. The boards come with one smooth side and one slightly rougher side.

A good example of where cementitious board is advantageous over render is in pebbledash. If you render over pebbledash, should the pebbledash fall off, the render will come with it. Rather than going through the laborious and often expensive process of removing pebbledash, it is possible to attach boards directly over the pebbledash, creating a stable surface.

UNUSUAL CLADDING MATERIALS

Here are some different ways to clad all (or part) of the front of your house. If you use the correct sealant protection, any number of materials can be considered for use.

- **Wallpapered panels.** You could wallpaper waterproof mdf boards and then coat the wallpaper in resin, which would seal out damp and protect the paper from the elements.
- **Car number plates.** These could be used as tiling on the front of a house.
- **Rubber.** You could fix this either as tiles or solid sheets.
- **Crushed glass, marbles or pebbles in mortar.** These are applied in a similar way to pebbledash.
- **Mirror.** Either as a mosaic or as strips on glass.
- **Printed hoardings.** It is possible to print large images and fix the fabric to the façade, as seen on elaborte building sites such as St Paul's Cathedral.

The intended zinc cladding for this house was too expensive so an exterior grade ply was cut to a fish scale pattern and then painted on both sides in a reflective silver paint, creating a convincing and textural finish that resembled metal.

METAL CLADDING

Metal sheeting and mesh are contemporary cladding materials often used on modern buildings, and you need to know the different types of metals that can be used on the front of your house and how to support them. How the panels meet is crucial to ensure a good effect.

When left in an untreated state, metals will rust and change their appearance. So unless you wish to encourage this process you need to use either galvanized steel, aluminium or stainless steel, or paint a protective coating over the metal. The metal will not be fire-resistant until it has been coated with a special paint.

Metal fixings also need to be considered for use externally. It is highly recommended to use stainless steel or at least galvanized fixings. Any other metal will rust over time, initially staining with a brown residue beneath the fixing and eventually breaking as the strength diminishes.

Stainless steel

This is strong but expensive. It can be bought in a number of finishes from polished to brushed matt.

Aluminium

This is lightweight and can be easily shaped, cut and coloured. It begins life as a very shiny silver but may oxidize over time to a duller grey. It is less expensive but not as strong as stainless steel.

Coretan steel

This is often used to expose the rusting nature of the steel, which changes to a soft orangey-red colour that is non-uniform over the surface and has an organic appearance.

Corrugated metal sheeting

This is inexpensive, which has promoted its widespread use as a roofing material, especially on industrial buildings. Used carefully, it can add a beautiful contemporary industrial style to a house design.

Metal mesh

An unusual metal cladding material, metal mesh comes in a range of styles and types, from fine sheets such as you would find in a kitchen colander to the type of mesh found on fencing. Meshes are an interesting material because they have a diaphanous quality that allows a glimpse of the surface underneath. You can get stainless steel meshes, galvanised steel meshes or those that have a plastic coating for protection. If you do consider cladding your house in metal mesh, think about how you will fix it to the building and allow for elements like window openings. Remember that metal can be very heavy in large quantities.

Copper

Often used as a roofing material, copper can also be used as a cladding. When exposed to the elements, it will change colour to a vermilion green known as *verdigris*; as can be seen all over Europe on state or church buildings. It is generally quite expensive but, if used in a small area or to highlight a feature, it can be very attractive. It has many of the same properties as aluminium.

Patination

It is possible to patinate many metals using a variety of techniques to achieve beautiful colours. Most of the processes apply heat, perhaps with another substance, to form a reaction. This results in the conversion of the surface metals into oxides. Once the desired effect is achieved, the metal is sealed using wax or varnish.

CASE STUDY
Cladding Larna's walls

Larna's house is a mid-terrace building with very little defining character from the other houses in the street except for its bold colours. The new design used the composition of the whole façade to break up the strong horizontal split that existed between the upper and lower storeys. Using four different types of cladding gave a modern, clean look to a rather dated building.

First the house was re-painted with a base colour of light grey, on to which a timber framework was fixed and painted. In the section surrounding the door and the three small hallway windows, horizontal strips of medium oak stained timber were added. To the rest of the house a stainless steel metal mesh was fixed in vertical panels to the timber structure. As the mesh is held away from the wall, all kinds of illusionary effects are created on the metal and the wall when the sun shines on to it.

The area around the door opening was then rendered to give a smooth, minimal surface. The door itself was clad with a sheet of copper which gives it a very effective green-blue patination.

Using all the different materials in subtle, innovative ways creates an overall effect of great tactility, both sheer and sleek.

SERVICES ON THE FAÇADE

Visible guttering and drainpipes are an element of the façade of most houses and must be worked into a design where possible. The water collected from the drainpipes used to be stored for times of drought, which is why sometimes you see very ornate lead rainwater square-section pipes just under the gutter as these were deemed very important parts of the building. Cheap cast-iron replaced lead and now cheaper plastic pipework replaces both. The plastic needs little maintenance, but is difficult to change colour as any paintwork will only have a limited life. Drainpipes are also available in aluminium.

On Eve Rowe's house (see page 106) the drainpipe and guttering was given a chrome finish in the style of shiny pipework found on some motorbikes.

Other elements that may be visible on the façade of your building may be a burglar alarm, vents, an extract from a boiler, ventilation bricks and meter boxes. In many cases it is important to maintain access to these items, so ensure that any cladding you apply does not cover over them.

ROOFS

Even though the main topic of this book is the front of your house and the front garden, it is worth touching on the subject of roofs. Houses can have projecting bays, balconies, porches and garages, all with some kind of roof. Their main job is to prevent water entering the property, and to limit the water falling down the façade to protect the lifespan of your house as well as to stop staining to the front or damp entering inside. This is why there is an overhanging eave (the base of the roof) with a gutter to collect the water and take it into the drainage system.

This waterfall feature made from slate effect tiles attached to a shiplap clad wall was a wonderful addition to this blank side wall. It gave the house a sense of nature and sounded fabulous as the water splashed down to the reservoir beneath it.

Roofs made of materials like thatch or tiles have the steepest slopes due to the small size of the individual component, whilst more homogeneous materials like metals or roofing felt can be laid practically flat. Each material has its own ideal pitch. Timber can be used to clad a roof and is found as timber shingles in oak or Canadian west cedar. This is light and durable and will weather to a silver-grey colour. Slate is a common cladding for roofs and lasts for hundreds of years. Lead is a type of metal that is used predominantly for roofing or flashing. It has a long lifespan and can be shaped easily and manipulated around corners and difficult junctions. Alternatives to lead are copper, aluminium, zinc, asphalt and bitumen felt.

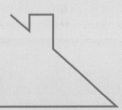

GREEN TIP
Other roofing products available today include rubber roofing tiles made from recycled rubber tyres which have been reformed into imitation slate; their visual appearance is indistinguishable from real slate.

Solar panel roof tiles are also sometimes incorporated into new buildings, generating energy to power the house.

FENCES AND BOUNDARY WALLS

The edge of a property defines the line between the public and semi-public domain.

This area has been known as 'defensible space' because someone is in controlled ownership of this space and because this reduces crime – the criminal is intruding even when on your front pathway. The way you choose to define the edge of your property depends on a number of factors. How secure do you feel in the neighbourhood? What kind of relationship do you wish to have with the street? How are you going to use your front garden? In other countries it is common for people to sit watching the world go by outside their front door or on the front patio or veranda. This would infer that the boundary fence is notional, a low edge that does not restrict the view.

If, however, you wish to have a more private relationship to the street, you may look to use hedges or planting, or building a fence or wall to define the boundary. Look at the various ways to use brick described earlier for interesting techniques for walls, or timber in order to weave a screen. Hedges can be cut into unusual designs. This is known as topiary – the pruning and training of a plant into a desired geometric or animal shape.

As a homeowner you will be faced with decisions on your boundary wall or fence. Boundaries are the most common form of dispute between neighbours and legal disputes are common. Therefore, it is advisable always to check the deeds of your house before erecting a new fence or wall and even possibly employing a qualified surveyor to peg out the boundary line – this may save on expensive legal bills later down the line. If you live in a terrace of houses then you are likely to have control of the fence on the left side only. This only applies if you are erecting a new fence, but not if you are only cladding or painting an existing fence.

A fence and gate can also be used to conceal items behind it, such as bins or cars. At Chris's house (see page 20) timber-panelled doors concealed the cars, and, similarly, Jason and Kate's house (see page 52) had a welded metal door to screen the area behind.

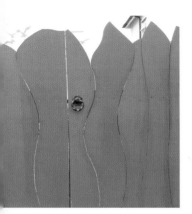

Far left: Nikki and Colin's front fence was made out of waney-edge timber and profiled to reflect the waves of the sea, continuing the theme of the house (see also pages 29 and 118).

Left: Zoe's fence utilized reclaimed timber floorboards of varying widths which were then painted to match the graphic colour scheme of the front of the house (see also page 44).

DOS AND DON'TS

DO

- Think about the scheme as a whole, including the front and sides of your property, before beginning work.
- Make sure you prepare the surface you are working on properly.
- Get suspicious cracks checked out first before covering them over or painting them in.
- Check the weather before starting painting or rendering work.
- Try to do as much preparation before fixing anything on to the façade. For example, paint both sides of cladding boards prior to installation.
- Think about all the details and junctions with the windows and doors before beginning work.
- Consult your neighbours before commencing work.
- Ensure that the materials you use are fit for the purpose; that the fixings are strong enough and will not rust.
- Think about how the materials will weather.
- Be careful to ensure your safety if you are climbing up ladders.

DON'T

- Try to cover over cracking or peeling paint, or loose render as your new surface will not adhere correctly to this.
- Attempt difficult cladding work by yourself unless you are sure of what you are doing.
- Clad over air bricks or ventilation openings; the house needs these to breathe.
- Undertake work without making the necessary checks for planning permissions.
- Erect fences over the legal height.

CHAPTER 6
LIGHTING
BY DAY
AND NIGHT

Lighting the exterior of your house is one of the most exciting ways to transform it. It is one of the key design tools that you can use to make a real difference and, after colour, one of the most satisfying. Light can create a strong aesthetic transformation and also has a number of key functional requirements that must not be overlooked: from welcoming guests to deterring would-be intruders. The lighting of your house falls into two distinct categories; natural daylight and artificial, and both play a key role. Take a fresh look at the light and shade falling on to your house in the daytime and at night. Can you see the house number from the street, find your keys at the front door, are there dark dangerous areas, does your garden lack magic and sparkle? Are you confused, baffled, or dazzled as to where to start to remedy these problems? Then read on!

THE IMPORTANCE OF LIGHT

Whatever beautiful designs you have created, without a light source to illuminate them, they cannot be seen and enjoyed.

By day the sun is our light source, modulated by the constantly moving clouds and giving a continuously changing and rather erratic, unpredictable light quality. By night we have to supply our own light. Except for the light reflected by the moon, we rely on artificial light to illuminate our houses, streets and roads. We have created complex lighting environments to ensure we can still clearly see up the garden path to the front door.

We also rely on lighting as a messaging service. Lights on inside a house are a sign that people are at home. A flashing light says 'watch out' or 'look at me'. This identifies a warning signal such as a police car, or an approaching bicycle. We all know the orange glow of a street lamp or the blinding light of a car headlight. We use coloured and flashing lights in connection with music at parties and celebrations. All these are familiar parts of our daily life.

Even on an overcast day there is sufficient reflected sunlight to ensure that we can see, but when the clouds appear and the sky turns grey we look to electric lighting to brighten up our surroundings once more. Light plays an important part in our health, too. In Seasonal Affective Disorder, society has recognized an illness that causes people to suffer psychological depression from a lack of sunlight. Just as plants need the sunlight to grow, so we react well when we are in well-lit, bright surroundings. All this means that it is important to think carefully about the effect lighting is having on your home – both from the inside and the outside – and on you.

So without much effort, you can transform your home when the sun sets. Lighting is not just about sticking a spotlight high on a wall and hoping for the best! Although utility lighting is important, light can be used to create very definite moods. Light certainly extends those daytime hours outdoors and adds a welcome atmosphere. Lighting can complement and focus any special features of your house or garden; it will control our eye movements and attention to its source. At the flick of a switch, with the help of some discreet sensors or even at regular timed intervals, the front of your home can become much more than just the path you walk up to reach the front door.

Good even street lighting is essential to create a sense of safety within a neighbourhood. Darker poorly lit areas will create a sense of anxiety. Even having lights on inside the houses give a greater sense of security to the street.

DAYLIGHT – WHAT TO CONSIDER

When thinking about lighting for your house, the first thing you should consider is the amount of natural light that comes in and how the transition from day to night affects your home.

The materials and colour applied to the front of your house will be strongly influenced by the amount of direct sunlight that falls on to the building. It is worth understanding the orientation of your house and how natural daylight affects the amount of light admitted into the interior. Does your front garden face north, south, east or west?

The sun rises in the east, bringing with it the early morning light, which has a warm, orange feel that is naturally invigorating. As it rises higher into the sky, we get daylight with a cooler, blue quality. The higher the sun is, the less directional the light will be – the sun is at its highest point at noon. The sun sets in the west and the light reverts back to warmer, orange hues. A rising or setting sun creates long shadows, the direction of which depends on the rise or fall of the sun. The amount of sunlight also depends on the season: there is less in winter, as the sun is lower in the sky than it is in summer.

A north-facing house does not receive direct sunlight and therefore undergoes a less dramatic transformation throughout the hours of the day. The light conditions of a south-facing house continually shift with the sun and the rays of infrared light from the sun cause surfaces to heat up. This may influence your window treatments if you wish to restrict the amount of sunlight entering the house. The sun's rays can also cause discoloration of a surface, material or paint finish over lengthy periods of direct exposure. This all

needs to be considered when choosing which colour to paint your house or the type of cladding materials to use.

If you are concerned about a lack of natural daylight entering your property you should first consider obvious factors such as making sure the window surfaces are regularly cleaned. Look to see if there are obstructions that are putting your house into shadow. There may be trees nearby that need pruning or large bushes or hedges that restrict light from entering the rooms or garden. Likewise, you should think about this aspect when planting out your garden; think ahead about the size a plant will grow to and which direction a shadow may be cast according to the orientation of your home and the placement of windows.

If privacy is an issue or you wish to restrict the amount of sunlight entering the front rooms, try to find ways to obscure vision without blocking out all the natural light. See 'Window Openings and Accessories' (pages 56–75) for detailed ways of doing this. To make more of any available light in your hallway a good option is to replace a solid door with a glass-panelled one – obscured glass will offer differing degrees of privacy depending on the pattern in the glass.

HOW TO MAKE THE MOST OF LIGHT

- Remove completely or partially unnecessary window coverings to allow more light into the interior
- Cut down bushes or trees obscuring the windows
- Paint window sills white / light colours
- Liven up north-facing façades by painting them a bright colour
- Add shading, such as plants or canopies, to south-facing façades
- Make sure lights are free from dirt and debris
- Clean your windows!

LIGHT AND COLOUR

If the front of your house is often without sun, you may find that it feels sombre and uninspiring. Mosses may grow, it may feel dark no matter what the weather and you will only be able to have shade-loving plants. Rather than letting this be a problem, use it to your advantage. Introduce bold or vibrant colours to resist the shadow and bring a sense of bright light and warmth. You could also look to places that could be romantic in shadow and create a shaded glen, as we did for Mark and Louise's house (below).

If the front of your house is shaded and you wish to give the illusion of natural light, there are several tricks you could employ. A sense of vibrancy can be achieved through patterning and colour highlights. An illusion of light and shade can be created with defined colours used against each other. We used this effect on the house that was designed for Hazel (see page 102).

Another trick to consider if your house is lacking light is to bounce light off the surface of other objects. By painting your window frames, sills and surrounds in white, you provide surfaces for light to bounce off and into the room. Shiny glossy surfaces will reflect a greater amount of light into a room. This effect can also be achieved by careful placement of light-coloured garden furniture, water features, or even mirrors.

In contrast, if you have a south-facing façade you may wish to use the changing light conditions. Any raised surface or object fixed to the façade will add a three-dimensional quality. Eve Rowe's house (see opposite and page 106), was given a patterned effect on the cladding panels of her house similar to motorbike spokes. These were formed using screws and stainless steel cables threaded to form the pattern raised off the surface. The effect of sunlight on the metal and the shadows gave a three-dimensional effect.

White or light-coloured houses work well at reflecting the sunlight to provide a bright environment. These colours also show up shadows from plants or objects that create a theatrical effect. Cooler colours such as blues work well on a sunny façade. Colour changes its hue considerably with the varying light conditions, so be careful when choosing finishes that match. Remember that bright sunlight will bleach colour, so a pale colour will often appear as white. With this in mind you can get away with using stronger colours. This is why many Mediterranean countries use bright pastels.

Left: Mark and Louise's north-facing house does not receive much natural light. Using mossy natural colours, a Celtic design was used to create a pattern on the house which is reminiscent of lichen growing on a wall. The design uses the romantic idea of a shady wooded Welsh glen, which works well with the lack of light.

Right: This house has UPVC ship lap boards that have been professionally sprayed in a tonal colour scheme. In addition to this, a decorative wire-work sculpture was positioned over the façade, that glints and shines in the sunlight, giving the house a dynamic daily transformation.

NIGHT-TIME: MAKING A STATEMENT WITH LIGHTING

As day ends and night draws in, artificial lighting is needed to replace sunlight.

Artificial light comes in a plethora of styles, colours and levels of intensity. You may ask why bother with the front of your house when it is not an area you normally spend time in? Lighting, however, can be functional as well as ornamental. If you take the time to redesign the front of your house and the front garden then why not allow this to be seen at night as well as in the day? In addition, exterior lighting is a fantastic way to add visual interest without the hassle of building works, and at the same time increases the security of your home. Think about trying to create a subtle, natural feel so that plants, pathways and features are painted with light.

Daylight gives equal lighting over the garden and house and therefore gives no priority to one area over another. Night-time becomes your chance to take control over the environment – it is an opportunity to bring depth and life to the external aspect of your house.

It is also worth considering the effect on the interior. During the day, the view out of the window adds considerably to the experience of being in a room. At night, what is seen through the window changes to a black mirror-effect. Clever outdoor lighting can eradicate this and visually expand the interior room by giving it an outdoor view. Lighting a planted garden area outside a window can make the garden feel like part of the room.

What is not illuminated can be equally important from a design perspective. Letting areas fall into shadow can hide less than perfect aspects of the exterior while adding an enhanced sense of depth and dimension.

The owner of this house was a boat-builder and the design picked up features from ships and the sea (see also page 27). The front door was painted a bright yellow, which attracts attention to the door during the day yet helps increase the luminosity of the front porch when lit at night. Two storm lanterns were fitted to highlight the entrance to the porch and provide a glow either side of the door. In addition, the side extension was clad with timber integrating the garage doors. Four portholes were added to light this area, all with frosted glass. Two of these had electric lights behind them, while the other two illuminate when the garage lights are turned on.

LIGHT POLLUTION

If light shines on to other houses or through neighbours' windows it is considered a form of pollution by the authorities. Light spilling beyond your property is known as light trespass, so it is important when aiming floodlights to make sure you only light the area intended. Check your directional lighting at night when you can see clearly the area that is being lit. If you are finding it difficult to control the angle and aim of your light, consider fitting a hood to the light to restrict it.

Security lighting is often installed without full consideration of its effect on neighbours and the environment. Domestic security lights should provide the minimum level of illumination necessary to light a property and draw your attention to potential intruders, but not to create an excess of light.

Some planning authorities have curfews for obtrusive lighting above a certain level, so it is always advisable to check with your local authority before installing exterior lighting. Although there are often no planning permission requirements imposed for lighting residential buildings, some authorities specify that all non-essential lighting, such as decorative floodlighting, should be switched off at a specified time.

APPROACHING YOUR LIGHTING DESIGN

Exterior lighting can produce an array of brilliant effects. The first thing to know is that people are drawn to the brightest source of illumination, so you can lead visitors to exactly where you want them to go. It therefore seems logical to place the most light at the front door. However, two common problems that occur are, firstly, that the homeowner places high wattage bulbs in the lamps by the front door which overpower the rest of the lighting; and secondly, security lighting with a motion sensor are placed on the garage door. These security lights are often harsh, confrontational and far from inviting. No one wants to shine a bright light in their visitors' eyes. Landscape lighting and security lighting serve two different functions. Neither one should negate the other.

It is worth remembering that exterior lighting has an impact on the view you'll see from inside your home. Windows act as picture frames for the outdoor view. If you wish to frame particular views from your windows then sufficient lighting is required. Poor lighting will create a mirror-effect on the window pane from inside, meaning that you will only be able to see yourself in the glass rather than seeing through it into your garden. Try to create a lighting level outdoors that is equal to or brighter than the indoors lighting level; it will eliminate the mirror-effect and make the exterior part of your interior room.

The first step in designing an exterior lighting system is to decide what you want to see outside and what you want to see from inside your home.

CASE STUDY
Edward Hopper colours

Hazel is an admirer of the work of Edward Hopper, an early 20th century artist whose paintings are famous for their use of particular hues that create long, deep-cast shadows.

The design of Hazel's house also creates the illusion of deep-cast shadows on the front and the side of the building. The existing porch was removed and an awning was added in its place. Awnings are usually used to shade an area from the sun but here the struture was also used as a graphic feature to create contrast and a play between light and dark on the front of the house. The lines created by the awning were intensified by strokes of colour. The overall design of the pattern created is abstract, but it fools the eye into considering that non-existent light sources are casting shadows on the façade of the building.

The colours used to express these imaginary light sources are inspired by those used by Edward Hopper in his paintings.

The concept is accentuated by the playful manner in which the metal number sign is projected on to the house beside the front door and then painted in as if it were a shadow.

Floodlights with barn doors (hinged metal baffles made by a local metal worker) were then positioned around the house and garden to transform it by night, casting a new series of oblique lines of light and shade to continue the illusion as night falls.

DIFFERENT TYPES OF LIGHTING

The secret of good lighting is not to have too much of it. The best lighting systems wash light around the garden so that you're not sure where it's coming from, and manipulate the light sources to create ambience and atmosphere.

Exterior lighting can be broken into four categories:

1 Security lighting
This is the most popular type of lighting used on the exterior of a building. Using timers and sensors, this lighting can be a valuable addition to home security.

2 Task lighting
This means functional light that enables activities such as seeing the path to the front door or illuminating the hot tub! If possible, you should be able to switch off these lights when they are not being used for their specific tasks.

3 Accent lighting
This highlights specific outdoor details. Good accent lighting will dramatically light up a small area so that it appears to glow from within. Always aim to hide the light source for this effect. Shielding the bulbs will help to eliminate glare.

4 Ambient (or general) lighting
This aims to provide sufficient illumination for any purpose. Ambient light is usually soft and flattering, filling a space rather than being directed at a particular function.

USING LIGHT TO SECURE YOUR HOME
Since man discovered fire, we have used light as a self-defence mechanism against animals and other predators. Today we are no different but use slightly more sophisticated means.

Well-positioned external lighting can be a very effective deterrent to potential burglars and other unwelcome visitors. Whether continuous or triggered by movement, lighting can provide a sense of security when approaching your home and when you are inside, although a continuous light source is a stronger deterrent than a light triggered by motion, as people rarely check when these are set off. Motion-triggered security lights should be positioned high so that they cannot be tampered with, ideally at a height of 2.75m (9ft). Their sensitivity should be set so that small animals and birds do not repeatedly set them off, and the sensor positioned so that it covers just your own property.

Many people install tungsten halogen floodlights because of price and ease of installation. These units can provide satisfactory security lighting if correctly installed and aimed, but it is rarely necessary to use a lamp of greater than 2000 lumens (150W) in these fittings. The use of higher power only causes more glare and darker shadows, affecting our ability to see and offering a convenient hiding place for criminals.

Bulkhead and porch lights are effective as they cast fewer shadows and so reduce hiding places for criminals. They can be fitted with a movement detector if required and so become both task lighting and security lighting. Porch lights are generally mounted lower than straightforward security lights and are therefore less susceptible to complaints from neighbours. An override switch can be added, if you like, so that you can choose whether you have them on, off or motion-triggered.

TASK LIGHTING

Task lighting refers to lighting that aids and facilitates an action. Otherwise known as practical lighting, it is important to get it right. You could use spotlights by steps to stop people tripping up in the dark, a porch light to allow you to find your keys and open the door in darkness and let you see who is outside, or security lights that are triggered by movement. Just because task lighting is practical doesn't mean it has to be unattractive. There is a large range of attractive contemporary exterior lights on the market. Consider looking at the range of shipping lights used for boats and barges. All these are water-resistant for external use. Safety lighting or inset floor lights such as on steps, pathways and patio edges can be used to enhance the front garden whilst creating a safer area at night for residents and visitors.

Pagoda lights are lights that stand proud from the ground. They come in a variety of shapes, sizes and materials and are possibly the most common lighting used for drives and pathways. For a more minimal look there are fittings available that are flush-mounted or recessed. These are weatherproof, suitable for driving over and can withstand impact. When buying a

These reproduction Georgian period lights reflect the spooky nature of the design and are highly functional due to the inbuilt PIR sensor that activates them.

product, ask about its IP (Ingress Protection) rating, which tells you about the product's ability to withstand a variety of factors – weather and water ingress. In general, exterior lights should be IP44 rated or more, but check suitability with the supplier before purchasing.

LED lighting technology has really taken off in recent years and there are many fittings for path and front door lighting. LEDs give a contemporary feel and can be inset flush into your pathway or doorstep. The glass plate in the top of the light is toughened glass that can be clear, opaque, coloured or even a recycled, crushed glass finish. The downside to LEDs is that they act only as guide lights rather than providing good illumination; halogen lighting for increased illumination is better.

Lighting your front door means using a form of porch light. When you are on the outside, a porch light will provide a sense of personal safety when returning to your home. Also, if you are inside your house you will be able to see any visitor illuminated through a glazing panel or spyhole in the door.

Porches vary in style and construction (see 'Porches', pages 50–51) so let the architecture dictate your choice of lighting. Some are enclosed and others simply a canopy over the door. If the porch is enclosed, for example, lighting inside will allow the porch to glow when seen. If the lights are concealed from view the porch will appear to have a uniform glow with no direct light source. This works well if frosted glass or film has been used on the windows to the porch. If the porch is attractive, illuminate its structure using inset floor lights and lower wattage concealed fittings under the porch to light the door. Porch lighting is often fitted with a bulkhead light using a low power (9/11-watt), compact fluorescent lamp. Their low-wattage means these lights can be left on all night to provide a constant sense of security.

Otherwise there are many other ways and means to light your porch. A suspended light could add to the drama, as could a shipping lantern such as in the Boat-builder house (see page 100). Authentic shipping lanterns are available for exterior use from sailing shops, but there are also many other reproductions available – always check that they are made of a material suitable for exterior use. If the inside of your porch is painted all one colour and lights internally, the porch will shine with this colour. Jason and Kate's dynamic circular porch (see page 52) was given a life of its own in this way. You could even create your own porch with lights as was done at Barry and Kerry's house (see pages 53 and 84).

FLOODLIGHTING

It is amazing how a garden can be transformed after dusk by the addition of a few well-chosen lights. If your house has a particularly interesting design it may add interest to the street if you use floodlights to light the façade. Floodlighting is generally used to display whole houses and large trees and requires heavy duty lighting. Floodlights come in a variety of sizes and intensities: some are directional, meaning that they can be focussed on a certain area. Most floodlights on the market are low-pressure sodium lights that come in a range of wattage, although halogens can also be used. It is normally unnecessary to use a lamp of more than 150 watts (2000 lumens), otherwise the lights may cause glare, create extreme shadows or cause light pollution and make you unpopular with your neighbours.

Floodlights get incredibly hot when left on for a long duration. In the front of house ensure these are out of the way of anybody touching or falling over them.

MINI PROJECT Lighting your house number

Consider making a lighting feature of your house number by creating it in light. Not only will this add an interesting design feature, but it will make it easier for visitors to find you.

Larna's house has a slick contemporary design that uses materials in a modern way. The house has clean lines and a sense of uncluttered elegance. As a feature of the house, a neon light was created in the shape of the number 20. The blue light of the neon is set against a darker blue painted background so the number appears to jump out from it.

CASE STUDY

Motorbike lighting

Eve's house had one obvious problem on first glimpse – the front door was tucked away down the side of the house. There was no focus to the entrance; if anything, the door appeared as a back door. The other hurdle was the strong horizontal UPVC – effect timber shuttering that connected the semi- detached properties. The design needed to tie into the existing structure while giving a distinct identity to Eve's house.

Eve was a lover of motorbikes, owning her own bike and having many pictures of the world of racing inside her house. Taking this on board, the house was given a motorcycle image in an abstract way.

The UPVC cladding continued down the entire length of the front wall and a central strip of it was added to the side wall, to frame the front door and bring a focus to the edge of the house.

A specialist company was brought in to spray a design onto the UPVC cladding that reflected the movement of flags the final lap of a race. The design was marked out by projecting it on to the house and masking the areas to be sprayed.

To further accentuate the front door, wing mirrors and car headlights were arranged around the door. These bounced the light around and provided not only the task lighting but also made a real feature of the entrance.

Other additions included a second layer of nails and cables arranged like spokes in front of the façade. The house was south-facing and received direct sunlight which caught the metal and provided continually shifting shadow patterns on the walls (see page 99). Finally the drainpipes were painted chrome, and circular ring curtains added to the interior.

FEATURE LIGHTING

Lighting the exterior of your home or your garden can create a magical scene. Lights can give emphasis to areas of the garden at night that would not be looked at during the day and simple feature lighting can create additional interest by lighting key features such as specimen plants, statues and trees, adding depth and interest to a garden or building at night.

Backlighting will silhouette a plant or structure against the light. Shadowing shows how light can be just as noticeable by its absence as by its presence. If you shine a light at an object at a particular angle, then the object's shadow will be thrown against a wall, fence or other surface. By moving the light closer or further away from the object you can alter the shape and size of the shadows too. This technique is often forgotten when it comes to creatively lighting the front garden or the front of a house. Lighting can pick out special features on the façade as well as the shrubbery. Washing light up or down a part of a wall can create interest and reveal a material in a completely new context. Alternatively, lighting can be used to highlight unusual brickwork, tiles or mosaic on the façade. Lighting can be concealed under the eaves of a house or used to outline the edges of a property, giving the building an interesting abstract quality.

Water feature lighting

Lighting a water feature can create a dramatic effect as water takes on the hue of the light source illuminating it. One thing to try to achieve is to keep the source of light hidden. The best location for a light that highlights a pool of water is on the side closest to where you will view it from – probably the house side of the water. This way you won't see glare but just a glowing body of water.

Another interesting combination of light and water is not to light the pool directly but to up-light surrounding trees and plants. This has the effect of turning the water into a mirrored surface reflecting its surroundings.

Still water should be treated very differently from other water features such as fountains where the water is usually chlorinated. Algae can easily become a problem in still water and will be highlighted if lights are placed inside the water shining out. In this case it is better to use the water as a reflecting pool. Have a look at 'Get wired for lights and water features', pages 130–131 for more ideas about how to light up water features.

Far left: Create a feature of your ornamental planting by lighting it to magical effect at night using concealed spotlights.

Left: Water features offer a great opportunity to create dynamic and kinetic sculptural pieces that really come alive at night; lighting under the water surface will create some illusion and accentuate the rippling surface.

CREATING LIGHTING EFFECTS

Lighting should be used to create an inviting feel. A technique called 'light layering' uses different lights to create subtle layers and does not draw attention to the light sources. Lighting some areas and leaving others in darkness can give a wonderful sense of depth to an outside area. Lighting objects and planting adds dimension.

A well-designed exterior lighting system gives all the required information about the space and flatters the residence and surrounding landscaping rather than overpowering it.

An effect known as 'moon lighting', which creates dappled patterns of light and shadow, can be created by attaching low-voltage lighting to trees or high points. The term comes from the glow that is created by a full moon. This effect is quite different from more traditional methods of outdoor lighting.

With low-voltage lighting, fixtures and bulbs can be so small that they disappear amongst planting, whilst also providing attractive illumination for particular areas.

Most low-voltage light fixtures use halogen light, which produces a more yellow light than daylight. Many lighting manufacturers now offer blue filters that are designed to eliminate the yellow. These are commonly known as daylight blue filters or colour-correcting filters. It is better to keep light levels at full brightness to maintain healthy looking, blue-white quality illumination. Plants can look unhealthy under yellow light, so if you want to achieve the effect of a lush garden you must colour-correct your lights. Dimmer lights will also emit an intensely yellow light and are therefore not a good choice for the same reasons.

WHITE LIGHT

This usually refers to a colour temperature between 5,000 and 6,250 degrees Kelvin, which is composed of the entire visible light spectrum. This light allows all colours from the visible light spectrum on an object's surface to be reflected, providing a light quality that is the same as daylight.

TIPS FOR LIGHTING EFFECTS

- Lighting can create the sense of an outdoor room when used well. Clever lighting will make use of trees, high fences, house eaves and other tall garden furniture such as pagodas and gazebos. These vantage points provide good structures for attaching lighting to.
- Downlighting creates a soft ambient light. Overlapping lights from different vantage points will reduce shadows and spread the light.
- Uplighting is used to create dramatic effects. Lights are aimed upward, usually towards a house façade or at trees and other vertical surfaces.

- Silhouetting creates a high-contrast effect where the foreground is left in darkness and the background is lit.
- Take care when using spotlights as they can easily dominate the view over an entire outdoor space.
- The best effect for path lighting is achieved when the light itself is not overly visible but the path is subtly highlighted.
- Moon lighting can be achieved by fixing lights above trees and plantings and pointing them downwards to create patterns and shadows whilst allowing through patches of light.

LIGHTS TO BE SEEN

While some lights are designed to be discreet, providing an effect without drawing attention to the light source itself, others are designed to be seen. There are a number of designers and manufacturers producing innovative products to help you liven up the exterior of your home. See 'Resources', pages 155–157, for some suppliers.

Exterior lights come in a variety of colours, or even in light-changing colours. Stunning visual effects can be created but be careful not to use too many different colours. Instead, accent particular trees, shrubs or ornaments for eye-catching effects.

Treat light fittings as components. They can be used together or in multiples and arranged or hung in different ways to achieve different looks. Tom Dixon's 'Jack Light' is a dynamic, unusual light which can be stacked to produce a light sculpture or just used singly as a bold statement.

Other designer lights are widely and cheaply available and will allow you to experiment with fun lighting outdoors. Mathmos produces a range of colour-changing lights which are rechargeable, waterproof and independent of cabling. Once charged they will last for five to six hours. Extremis makes an exterior lighting product called 'Inumbra', which is like a pole of light that can be leant seemingly casually against a wall, hung or placed strategically. Used as components, they can be placed imaginatively to provide a different effect each time you use them. Metalarte has produced a range of contemporary lights that imitate the more traditional-looking standing lights that are used indoors. Made in moulded polyethylene and rechargeable, they give an indoor feel to outside.

Most of these lights are intended for use outside but it is worth checking whether they can be left outside for extended periods.

Left: These large nail like lights create a feature in themselves set within a minimalist setting, supplementing the spotlights to produce a bright light filled space.

Right: The soft glow produced by these paper bag candle lanterns compliments the magical effect created by the clusters of fairy lights; a wonderful if temporary effect for a special occasion.

LIGHTING FOR AN OCCASION

Using exterior space will open up the boundaries of your home beyond its walls, creating a whole new environment. A cleverly laid-out exterior space can function as another room that is specially dedicated to personal enjoyment and entertainment. If you are having a celebration inside the house then why not welcome your guests with a celebratory lighting design on the entrance to your home?

If you don't want to install a permanent display, put up temporary lights for a special occasion. We have all seen houses that are completely covered in Christmas lights, but it is possible to create some stunning effects that are slightly more toned down, whilst still showing that you have made an effort!

Most temporary exterior lighting is formed on a string or net, like outdoor fairy lights. This can be very effective as they can be wrapped around features such as trees and plants. String lights also come in a variety of designs and colours, ranging from miniature Chinese lanterns to stars.

As with permanent lighting, you will need to make sure that temporary lighting is correctly and safely installed. Ensure that there are no cables that people can trip over and that the lights are

Far left: This fire-pit was installed in Ange & Lee's garden. The large metal dish keeps a fire contained, preventing it from spreading or leaving a damaged spot in the garden. It is also a beautiful object in its own right which, when lit, has a stunning effect.

Left: Multiples of objects, such as these hanging oriental lanterns, will make any event feel special, as they sway gently in the breeze.

connected to a safe electricity supply that is nowhere near water.

Solar lights have become very cheap and widely available. One advantage of these lights is that they are self-sufficient, but the light they give off is very weak and the supply of energy that they gather throughout a day may only sustain them for a couple of hours. As a result, these lights can often be a false economy.

Naked flames are another possibility for lighting your garden. A controlled bonfire, for instance, will provide both light and heat. To avoid spoiling the garden, make sure you create a base. A specially designed fire-pit (as above) or wood burner, such as a ceramic chimney, can be used repeatedly, and will not damage your garden.

You can even buy iceboxes that feature an internal light, providing a fun and functional light source for a party!

CANDLES AND LANTERNS

Candles designed for outside use can be used to light areas of a garden. Take special care not to position them near potentially flammable objects, such as wood and leaves. Garden candles usually come on large sticks, which can be stuck into the ground and will provide light for a couple of hours. You may choose to have a few positioned along the garden path for a dramatic entrance to a party. If you have a pond in the garden, then floating candles can create a very pretty effect as they drift around in the water.

Outdoor lanterns are also widely available – these are usually oil-burning and different oil mixtures can be used to give off scents. If you find mosquitos annoying, try oils that contain citronella, which is a natural mosquito-repellent. Lanterns can be placed around a tree or hung from the branches. Wrapping a wire handle around the top of a jam jar and placing a nightlight candle inside is a cheap and easy way to achieve a similar effect.

PLANNING YOUR SCHEME

Whether lighting the garden or exterior of the house, good planning is essential.

First you must decide between stand-alone and wired lighting. Stand-alone lighting is normally solar-powered and is ideal as a quick solution to create ambient lighting. However, a solar power supply is not ideal if the light is to be positioned in densely planted borders. Wired lights require the installation of cables and power from the house. However, they will provide a reliable source of light which can be tailored exactly to your needs and can allow you to totally transform an exterior space.

THE PRACTICALITIES

The first step in planning an exterior lighting system is to decide exactly what you want, what effect you would like to achieve and which fittings will do this. Then you'll need to plan out how to make the electrical system work, and put the circuit together.

The lighting system will need to run from the main fusebox in the house. How much lighting you wish to install will determine how many circuits you need. If you have more than one circuit you can switch different lights on or off to suit the occasion.

To power exterior lighting, armoured cable will have to be buried deep into the ground, which may require you to dig up part of your driveway, garden or paving. Alternatively, you can run the wiring in a plastic or metal trunking at low level along a fence or low wall.

With electrical installations almost any amount of light is possible but the cost of the system will vary dramatically depending on the size of the area and how many circuits and fittings are needed. When buying the lights, make sure that the fittings have been designed for exterior use.

When planning the system, think about where would be the most convenient place for switches. A switch will need to be located somewhere along the run of the cable or by the house. For the front garden it is often best to have a light source that can be operated by a switch indoors, a sensor or by a timer.

Consult a qualified electrician and talk through the options and costs before going ahead; he or she will be able to advise you at this stage if your system would benefit from any adjustments.

TECHNICAL PLANNING

Lighting position

When designing, it is best to adopt a flexible approach. In practical terms this involves laying enough cable so that the position of the lights can be moved once the effects can be seen. Your lighting system can then be adapted as your garden plants mature. If possible, lay cables and irrigation pipes at the early stages when the front garden is being constructed to avoid having to dig trenches later on. Once the garden is created and the cable laid, it's a good idea to experiment with some temporary lights such as oil-filled lights or large candles. This can often produce some new and unexpected effects that you can then replicate using permanent fittings.

Installation

Safety is always a key consideration. Use an accredited electrician to install lighting; they will always ensure the system has a circuit-breaker or an electrical trip. For a 240-volt exterior lighting system, armoured cable will be laid underground where possible. This will be at a depth that allows for disturbance to the soil such as digging or forking. With all types of lighting it is a good idea to dig the trenches and lay the cables yourself but to employ the services of a qualified electrician to carry out the joints and connections. Doing the trenching work will save the electrician time in the installation, which will save you money. The electrician will advise you on which cable to use (this varies depending on the circuit), how deep and where to lay the cable.

You may find that you also need to position a transformer – a watertight electrical box – outside, depending on the system you require. The location of the transformer will also need to be determined by your electrician. The box can easily be disguised by planting.

USEFUL ELECTRICAL ORGANISATIONS

- **NICEIC (The National Inspection Council for Electrical Installation Contracting):** The NICEIC is the industry's independent safety regulatory body. It has a technical helpline and will point you in the right direction for further advice. Tel: 0870 013 0431
- **IEE (Institute of Electrical Engineers):** The IEE is an independent body that sets wiring regulations. It also has an advice line. Tel: 020 7240 1871
- **Lighting Industry Federation:** Tel: 020 8675 5432
- **Light Association:** Tel: 01952 290905

Draw up a plan of where your lighting cables lie for future reference in case you want to add more fittings to your current system.

Electrical codes vary from place to place, so always seek advice from a qualified electrician who is experienced in outdoor lighting. If you decide to do the work yourself, check with your local electrical inspector to see what is required. Try to use an electrician who is NICEIC (National Inspection Council for Electrical Installation Contracting) approved, to make sure that your lighting meets technical and safety standards.

WHERE TO FIND GOOD FITTINGS

An electrician who specializes in outdoor lighting systems will be able to advise you where to find appropriate light fittings. There are many manufacturers producing a wide range of quality products (see 'Resources', pages 155–157). Lighting should be viewed as a tool with which you can use to create numerous effects depending on what you want to achieve. Don't feel limited to the exterior lights on offer at your local DIY store; contact specialist light manufacturers and obtain some catalogues.

If you feel daunted by the variety of lighting on offer you could always ask a lighting consultant to design a system for you. Lighting consultants have the expertise to know how much light you need and how each light fitting will behave in a particular environment. Going down this route can be expensive, but it will usually guarantee a good result.

LIGHTING DOS AND DON'TS

DO

- Spend some time thinking about outdoor lighting during the initial phase of designing. This will prevent you having to put in a lighting system after completion of the other parts of the design.
- Use general, task and accent lights to create a balanced scheme.
- Use infrared sensors (PIRs) to activate lights when they are needed, and save electricity when they are not.
- Guide visitors to the front door with light, make them feel welcome.
- Consider light pollution from your lighting scheme.
- Make the most of your house's architectural features and those in the front garden with an inspired lighting scheme.
- Get your lighting installed by a qualified electrician.
- Have fun with your lighting!

DON'T

- Create glare by using too strong a light bulb in a fitting.
- Point lights towards people, which has the effect of obscuring rather than highlighting features.
- Use underwater lights in ponds as they will highlight algae and creates a dirty look.
- Allow debris to build up in light fittings.
- Use security lights for landscape lighting, as it will overpowers all effects.
- Choose out of proportion fixtures which highlight negative aspects of your house or garden.
- Use yellow light (halogen) without a daylight filter or it will produce a yellow effect.
- Let plants grow over fixtures and obscure the light.

CHAPTER 7
HARD LANDSCAPING

Designing your front garden has to start with the hard landscaping because without the paths, paving and driveways, the garden can't be planted. The design has to tie in with the façade of the house, so your cue should be either the look of your house as it stands, or as you've decided to design it. The most important thing is to be adventurous. Just because two-thirds of driveways are made from grey concrete, that doesn't mean yours can't be as different. Once you know what materials are available the more diverse you can be, whether you use a colourful resin-bond for the drive or fake turf for the lawn. Don't forget that your front garden isn't just a style statement – it's about making a place that you can feel comfortable in. Whatever design you choose, good luck and enjoy it!

REVOLUTIONIZE YOUR FRONT GARDEN

In the last ten years, the domestic British garden has been revolutionized. The back garden is no longer just a garden, it's an 'outdoor room', an extension of the home with something for all the family, including brand-new materials and features, like decking and hot tubs.

What we used to call a pond has become the 'water feature', and almost anything you care for can be bought instantly in containers, including ready-grown mature plants.

Meanwhile, front gardens have been largely ignored, trailing behind in the fashion stakes, failing to reach their potential. Even though the front garden provides the first impression to the outside world, it's usually the last place to be sorted out, after the inside of the house and the back garden. Front gardens have vast potential for purposes both aesthetic and functional – whether you just want to create a pretty, welcoming picture that complements you and the façade of your house, or you need a large driveway for two cars. But why not take it further? Visiting gardens around the UK for *Front of House*, it has really struck me how people struggle when trying to make the best of tiny back gardens, when they have huge untapped resources at the front.

If the front garden is fairly private, what's to stop you creating an entertaining area out there? Provided you attend to security and make sure furniture is pinned down, it's very feasible.

Or if the garden is really just one big driveway, it doesn't mean it has to be a barren sweep of concrete. There are many more interesting materials for a drive that offer the opportunity to make it look attractive *and* functional. But perhaps the hardest front gardens to design are those that have no real use – except as a passage to the front door. Instead of thinking of it as a problem, view it as an opportunity; this is space that does not have all the traditional pressures of the back garden, where everything from the pets to the patio has to be given consideration.

And last but by no means least, the garden is a wonderful foil for your house, your biggest investment and the outward representation of who you are. You enjoy spending time choosing materials that suit your needs and personality inside the house, and you might well have done the same outside at the back – don't miss the opportunity to have fun personalizing the front garden too.

A perspex screen makes a colourful and privacy-enhancing divide between the lawn and driveway in this Manchester front garden. When the sun shines during the day the screen casts stained-glass colours on the gravel behind; at night, uplighters accentuate the feeling of seclusion and create a party feel.

GETTING STARTED

If you've come unstuck trying to find ideas for the front garden, it's understandable. Designing the front garden is harder than designing the back, largely because it's a thoroughfare.

The front garden is a means of getting to your front door and somewhere to park the car and bins – hardly a good starting point. Also, there's that worry about fitting in with the rest of the street, and picking materials that don't clash with either your house or your neighbours' properties. So, rather than worrying about what style or plants you want in the front garden, focus on function. Start by asking yourself what is your front garden there for? Simply to park the car? Is it just a glorified path to the house? Or is its purpose to create a good impression and be an attractive foil for the house? Answer those questions and those in the list below, then ask yourself one final question: what more can it do?

There's no reason to let the potential of all that space at the front go to waste. It's your property, you paid for it, so make the most of it by making a vow to start thinking of it as your living space, every bit as much as the back garden.

Show off your best assets by marrying the style of your garden to the house. Here, natural colours and materials on the house façade suggest plenty of soft landscaping – hedges, turf, copper and wooden sleepers – will be in keeping.

QUESTIONS, QUESTIONS...

What is in the front garden at present?
Assess the aspect. Is it mostly shady or sunny? Is it private and quiet, or noisy and open to the road? Use a garden fork to check out the soil and, if necessary, buy a pH kit from the garden centre to give you an idea of the range of planting. Consider the services. Are there any overhead cables that could limit tree planting or manhole covers with underground pipes that might limit excavation? Assess existing planting. Is it any good? Are lawns and hedges in good nick? Can they be rejuvenated. Are there plants you hate that must go?

What is the location like?
What are the other houses and gardens like? If the area's very uniform, you may not want to stray far from the look, but if there are lots of different styles and paint colours, you have wider scope to be individual.

What do you want to use the front garden for?
Decide what you want to use the garden for. If parking is the main consideration, how many cars/other vehicles will need to be parked there?

What potential is there?
The size, the privacy, the view, the aspect, the shape and the existing hardscape may all suggest a use.

What style are you after?
Do you have a strong personal style that you'd like reflected in the garden? Any favourite colours, interests, materials? Do you prefer shabby chic or French formality? Are you interested in visual arts or prefer sports?

You don't just have to think along the usual garden themes of Japanese, Mediterranean or cottage, unless you want to. Keep the final look of the house in mind as the front garden and the overall look should work together rather than vying for attention.

How will it happen?

Think carefully about who would do the work. Do you need someone to work out the quantities of materials? What's the timescale? Do you need planning permission? Are there any obstacles to storing or bringing in materials, such as restricted access? Do you need to notify the neighbours or, if you're intending to leave stuff on the public footpath, your local council?

DESIGNING AND DRAWING IT UP

Doing a drawing on paper doesn't suit everyone – some people prefer to work on the ground. But if you're handy with a pen and paper, try making a scale drawing to see if your ideas work on paper first. As well as a 10–30m (33–100ft) tape to measure the plot, you'll need a scale ruler, A3 drawing paper, pencils and an eraser; a compass and set square are handy but not essential. It's convention to use a scale of 1:50 and it helps to know certain standard measurements. For example, paths are usually 900mm (3ft) wide; driveways need to be between around 3m (10ft) wide and 5m (16½ft) long to accommodate one car; patios need to be around 2–3sq m (21½–32sq ft) to comfortably seat four people; and steps and areas around doors should be bigger than paths because these are areas where people tend to gather. Very small areas of lawn, less than 3sq m (32sq ft) or very fiddly shapes, are a pain to mow and will need specialist trimmers or hover-mowers.

Don't be afraid to declare your passions in the front garden – here a motorbike enthusiast's garden gets a racing look with a track-style path and bespoke water feature.

PLANNING

You'll probably know if you live in a Conservation Area or a listed building, which will restrict work on existing trees and boundaries. Individual trees may also be the subject of Tree Preservation Orders and you'll need permission before undertaking work on them. Check out who owns the boundaries – the information will be on title deeds or you can check with your solicitor. For a small charge, you can get copies of your deeds from HM Land Registry (www.landreg.gov.uk). Occasionally, title deeds include restrictions on what you can do in the front, such as keeping the garden open plan or not allowing a front boundary. In theory, you need planning permission when building a wall or fence more than 1m (3½ft) high next to a public highway or public footpath and more than 2m (6½ft) high on other boundaries. Hedges require no planning permission, although legislation is in the pipeline that will give local councils power to keep hedges to 2m (6.6ft) if they restrict light to another property.

Attention to details in the early stages of planning and even discussing your plans with neighbours can save a lot of agro later on, and may even give you scope to take your plans further than you'd hoped.

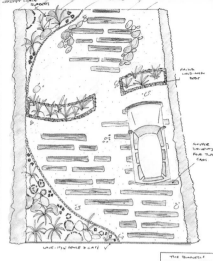

CASE STUDY
Planning a Beachcomber garden

Before the *Front of House* team turned up, this Norfolk garden was just a gravelled driveway, overwhelmed by two large leylandii hedges along the boundaries. Neat, functional, but boring was how their friends described it – unlike the young, vibrant couple who lived there and in no way matching the shabby chic used for the interior. We decided a beachcomber look was perfect, reflecting their love of natural materials, coastal walks, and the house's proximity to the sea.

In terms of function the garden couldn't change that much as the Bunwells still wanted to park two cars on it. The width of the garden isn't much bigger than two cars side by side, so my solution was to create a forked driveway to avoid stacking the cars up side by side or one behind another. Exchanging the existing gravel for a darker local flint created a better contrast

with the house and a sympathetic feel, while allowing for staggered sleepers to be sunk into the ground to demarcate the drives. I chose reclaimed wooden sleepers to suggest seaside groynes, and created a full-stop at the end of the two drives with staggered planters made of gabions, similar to the metal mesh used as sea defences. Large pebbles filled the sides of the gabions, along with coastal paraphernalia found at a local salvage yard, including lovely big rusty bolts, anchors and huge links of iron chain. Because the garden was north-facing, I went for shade-loving dogwoods and a smokebush to create privacy near the road, with cascading stipa and berrying cotoneaster for the planters. The borders were edged with wood to stop the gravel spilling onto the soil and clad with a length of rusty iron chain for that harbour feel.

LOOKING FOR INSPIRATION

With a host of hard landscaping themes to pick from, it helps to narrow down the features and appropriate materials by focusing on a look that reflects your tastes. This could borrow from a landscape or holiday destination that's close to your heart, or reflect a hobby or preferred style of clothing. You can introduce the theme throughout the garden or just use it subtly, in the furniture or containers, for example.

TEN SOURCES OF STYLE INSPIRATION

1. Personal interests

If you love aromatherapy, reflect it in the planting with plants such as essential-oil filled lavender and rosemary. If you're mad-keen on dancing, introduce a motif of the style of dance as at the Art Deco House (see pages 14 and 124). Eve Rowe's fascination with motorbikes was reflected in a circular water feature; made from toughened glass and etched in the shape of the spokes of a wheel, it picked up on Oliver's wire pattern on the front of the house (see pages 99 and 106).

2. History

Do you have a favourite period in history or are there aspects of your home that suggest a period style? Perhaps a colonial garden complete with rectangular beds, box topiary and pea gravel would suit you, or a Victorian kitchen garden, edged with marigolds and nasturtiums.

3. Favourite colours

Why not use your garden for colour therapy and restrict the shades of plants and hard materials to your favourites? Or try and make a close colour match with the shades of the bricks. This worked well with the planters at Tracy Wilson's Leafy

Plants by your front door should make you feel that you've come home, so what better welcome than a pair of standard olive trees for an Italian family who want to create a little bit of the Mediterranean in Manchester.

House (see page 86) where mahogany-leaved leucothoe was selected for the woven planters to match the hot paprika colour of the house brick. Similarly, the Mediterranean house (see page 152) stuck to the colours of the landscape, using buff-coloured paving and glinting blue glass as a mulch beneath the mature palm tree.

4. Nature

Want to commune with nature in your front yard? Choose stone from your favourite hills, or craft wooden totems and furniture to remind you of familiar woodland walks. The natural patriotic theme of Louise and Dave's Celtic House (see page 99) suited the local blue pennant slate perfectly, while another Cardiff home, the Waterfall House (see page 129) used slate to stack the gabions seats, which Dave and Tracy used to take in their amazing view out over the Welsh countryside.

5. Abroad

Every region has at least one strong style, whether it's Scandinavian pine, American Shaker or oriental minimalism. Show your interest by growing plants from the region; for example, Japanese maples for an Eastern look, or incorporate the colours of the flag. At the Diamond House in Manchester (see page 70 and above) Jeanette's Italian roots were reflected in a pair of olive trees by the front door, lavender hedges and a large entertaining area for the family to get together and eat their mama's wonderful home-made bolognaise.

6. Your personal look

Do you dress in particular style, say punk, New Age or Gothic? There's no reason why your front garden needs to be conventional if you're not. Committed Goths Ange and Lee looked far more at home when their front garden (see page 19) had been transformed into an eery horror-movie space, complete with a misty pond and wrought-iron fence. The wooden bench had a foot-rest chiselled out, blow-torched and stained with dark-brown paint to look like a Medieval stocks.

7. Parties and fun

Devote the front garden to enhancing your leisure time, a place where you can exercise, or practise golf or croquet. The English with a Twist garden (see page 20) combined formality with a series of rectangular putting greens, great fun for both grown-ups and kids. The owners of the Hopper house (see page 102), Neil and Hazel Lui, love partying and have a wide group of young friends who frequently visit for dinner parties and entertaining, plus a hedged garden with an area on the side – perfect for a sunken hot tub courtesy of *Front of House*!

8. Contemporary architectural

Look to modern architecture and the favoured materials of contemporary architects for your inspiration, such as glass bricks and stainless steel. If you feel uncertain about using hard materials, use turf and earth-scaping. Creating strong shapes in grass and soil looks very modern and yet doesn't jar with the wider landscape.

9. Family space

Make it a space where the whole family can relax, combining play areas with entertaining and sunbathing. At the Beach House in Cardiff (see below), the interior of the house made little distinction between grown-up areas and space for the kids, and this was reflected in a giant ice-cream patio which incorporated paving for the grown-ups, as well as a sandpit hidden beneath the deck, a see-saw and a soft play area made of recycled rubber mulch.

10. Art

Check out craft fairs and garden shows for local craftswomen and men who make bespoke boundaries and furniture in a style you like. You could commemorate the style of your favourite artist or period in the garden, as we did at Kerry and Barry's garden in Manchester (see page 84 and 115), recreating an early 20th century look that echoed the paintings of Mondrian.

Strong patterns work well where you have a view down onto your front garden, as at this seaside plot. An ice-cream shaped patio hid a sandpit and toy storage for the kids.

GETTING STARTED – PRACTICALLY

When making over your front garden you need to decide how much or little of the work you're going to do, and then delegate according to your time, skills and budget.

You might be thinking of the work just as building the paths or fences, but really the hard landscaping is just part of the work. If you are planning to do the whole lot, here's how it might roughly break down. You could choose to bring in a designer to do the first five points, landscape contractors to do the second five, and landscape gardeners (or sometimes the designer) to do the last two. Alternatively, you may save on money by undertaking part of the work yourself.

BREAKDOWN OF THE WORK
- Measure up garden
- Design garden
- Specify materials
- Quantify materials
- Source materials
- Organize storage of equipment and materials during the work, or if work is staggered, the sequence in which materials are needed
- Set a start date for when the work is going to be done and order materials
- Book skip
- Book any necessary hire tools such as turf lifter, plate vibrator and hedge-trimmers
- Start work – clearing existing hard landscaping, lifting turf, to leave you with a clean slate
- Start work on hard landscaping
- Planting and aftercare
- Draw up a maintenance schedule for pruning and trimming

GETTING AN IDEA OF THE WORK

If you've not done any landscaping before, the work can seem overwhelming, but there are ways of making it easier.

Lifting turf
If you've more than a couple of metres to lift, always hire a turf lifter from a hire shop. Basically it's a powered machine with blades set to just below the level of your turf which trundles along lifting the turf. You then just roll it up and compost it.

Removing paving
How difficult a job you have depends on how the paving was laid in the first place. If it's uneven, chances are it's just laid on sand and it'll be easy to lift. Either way, a pickaxe is useful for levering up slabs. Make moving them easier by 'walking' them to the skip on their edges. Concrete will need pick-axing out, or you may have to hire a drill. Drilling concrete isn't hard; the trick is to keep chipping away at the edges. But wear ear-defenders.

Removing trees and hedges
You need to hire a tree surgeon for trees bigger than 4.6m (15ft) or so, as the tree will need taking down in pieces with a chainsaw. Conifer hedges are hard work to get out but not impossible for a couple of burly types, as conifers are shallow rooted. Cut off the bushy stuff first, then leave 0.6–0.9m (2–3ft) of stump to help you lever out the roots.

Taking out fences
With panel fencing in poor repair, you may well need to only remove the worn panels, leaving the fence posts in place. Then it's just a matter of checking the measurements, ordering the panels and slotting them in place. To enhance their life, use gravel boards at the base to keep panels off the ground and prevent the wood from rotting.

QUICK TRICKS TO GOOD-LOOKS

If you'd rather make just cosmetic changes, here are a few tricks guaranteed to give your front garden the appearance of being cared-for. They can be done over a few hours or the course of a weekend.

- **Paint concrete fence posts and gravel boards.** Ugly off-grey, concrete fence posts and gravel boards spoil the look of the fence. Paint them in the same colour as the fence to tone them down and create a unified fence.
- **Re-shape the lawn.** Giving the lawn a strongly defined edge is one of the quickest ways to make a garden look more structured. For straight edges, peg a line of string between two bamboo canes close to the ground, then use the edge of a spade or ideally a half-moon edging tool to cut away the straggly edges. For curvy edges, cut using the same method except use a hosepipe or ground-marking paint as your guide.
- **Put an edging in around gravel.** Unretained gravel spills onto surfaces nearby and looks messy. A quick method is to use featheredge wooden board or 2x1in timber batten screwed to 8in pegs knocked into the ground, then painted to match the colour of fences.
- **Make stuff match.** Colour is a quick and easy way to make gardens look thought-through, so make sure that fences and gates are all stained the same colour woodstain.
- **Bring fence panels to the same height.** Don't allow the height of fencing panels to be higgledy-piggledy. If the ground slopes, step the fence but ensure the steps are even. Use gravel boards at the base to make the top of the fence look level and neat.
- **Show hedges who's boss.** Don't let overgrown hedges take over your garden. Most hedges, with the exception of leylandii and chamaecyparis conifers can take hard cutting back. Although they will look dead and twiggy for the first few months, once the green starts to grow back you will have potentially claimed back 60cm (2ft) or more of your garden.

WHERE TO BUY MATERIALS

All the suppliers we used on the series are listed at the back of the book (see pages 155–157), but if you want materials closer to home, these are the best places to look:

- **DIY Stores.** The large homeware stores stock a basic range of plants, concrete paving, containers, gravel and tools.
- **Builders' merchants.** For aggregate and paving materials.
- **Metal fabricators.** Provide mild and stainless steel, copper and aluminium in sheets, cut to size or welded to your specification.
- **Garden centres.** Stock more than just container-grown plants, containers, edging materials and water features.
- **Stone merchants.** Sometimes attached to local garden centres and builders' merchants. Local stone merchants will stock local stone sympathetic to the area and carriage will be cheaper. Track down stone merchants on the internet for a wider range of stone and nationwide delivery.
- **Timber merchants.** Local sawmills offer a wider range of wood products and will cut pieces to your specification.
- **Glaziers.** Your local glazier provides clear, frosted and coloured toughened glass suitable for outdoors and will cut it and etch it to your design.

DRIVEWAYS

Driveways are useful features for front gardens, creating a safe place off the road and adding value to your home.

Driveways don't have to be boring. Choice of materials makes all the difference, such as colourful resin bonded aggregates, which are brilliant for adding colour and interesting patterns.

In garden terms, though, they can look pretty stark – emphasizing the hard aspect of the house rather than softening it and making it feel part of the wider landscape as a planted front garden would do. This is particularly the case with block paving driveways, although it needn't be so if pockets are left on the edges for softening plants and climbers.

Hard landscaping a driveway is something that most people leave to the professionals, and for good reason, as it's a lot of work entailing:

1 Digging out the area to a depth of at least 150mm (6in) and filling the trench with a foundation of hardcore. This is to take the weight of vehicular traffic.
2 Keeping the edges, usually with kerbstones or pavers to retain the surface material. This is especially important with loose aggregate drives.
3 Surfacing, whether with pavers, slabs, gravel or a bonded material like concrete or tarmac.

If you want to do it yourself, the simplest surface to create is a loose aggregate or chippings, but you'll still need the depth of hardcore beneath or the car will sink into the soil, creating unsightly potholes and much wheel spinning! Choose a spar-style gravel over beach pebbles of between 6–10mm (¼–⅓in) as these have angular edges which lock to form a more solid surface. You'll also need to retain the edges with kerbstones or chunky timber to stop the stones spilling out. Loose chippings are not a good idea for drives on steep slopes – bonded surfaces like concrete or tarmac are more suitable.

DEALING WITH DRIVEWAY LAYOUTS

While you have options on the design of materials for the drive itself, you probably won't have much choice about where the drive is situated, unless you have a very large front garden. There are generally four typical layouts of how the drive relates to the rest of the garden, and this should be your first consideration when deciding on a design.

1 **The whole-garden drive**
The usual layout for narrow terraced houses where the front garden boundaries are set by the width of the house. Create a visual full-stop between the drive, the rest of the garden and the house. (See the Beachcomber garden, page 118.)
2 **Drive in the middle, with two areas either side**
This is often the case with houses on corner plots. Link the three separate areas together by using the same materials.
3 **Drive to the side**
This is the easiest to design because it looks and feels separate to the garden, so you can either include it in the design of your front garden or play it down, so it recedes visually. Alternatively, if the garden is small you can make it feel bigger. (See above and the English with a Twist house and garden, pages 20 and 142.)
4 **Sweep in front of the house**
With larger frontages, the driveway often curves round and sits diagonally across the front of the house. This creates the problem of taking up most of the garden, leaving only small, awkwardly shaped areas for the garden proper. (See the Rock 'n' Roll Garden, page 52.)

CREATING A NEW DRIVEWAY

The following factors should all be taken into consideration if you are planning to construct a driveway:

Cost

You should allow for the cost of the materials and, if you're hiring contractors, the labour. Also include the cost of changing the access from the road, such as widening the driveway or dropping the kerb.

Planning issues

Can you accommodate a car on your driveway? You should allow a minimum of 2.4m (7.9ft) wide by 4.8m (15.7ft) in length for each car. If there isn't an existing driveway, and your garden butts up to a pavement, you'll need to have the kerb dropped to allow access across the pavement. Check with the planning department of your local authority to see whether you need permission (this is only normally the case on main roads), then check with the Highways Department, who will either undertake the work and charge you for it or provide a specification for your own contractor to do the work. The Highways Department normally charges a small supervision fee, plus the cost of the contractor, which varies around the UK from a few hundred pounds to over £1,000 depending on the size of kerb and the area.

Design

The design will be restricted by the size of your front garden and the amount and size of the vehicles you're intending to park there. If you want to change where the driveway is in relation to the road, this could incur extra cost in moving gates, dropping kerbs and so on. Other choices relate to colour, pattern, materials and shape.

Where there is more than one car, it isn't always necessary to park both side by side, or in a line. Creating a forked driveway can look more attractive and allows for more shapely borders around it. It might be necessary to incorporate screens or markers to make a visual full-stop between the drive and the rest of the garden.

Materials

These will be dictated by budget, the look you're going for and the colour you want. Colour-wise, it's best to either harmonize with the colour of the house or go for a complementary shade that will contrast with and set off the colours of the house.

Who's doing the work?

For anything other than a gravel drive, use landscapers. Get estimates from local contractors and be sure to nail down the timescale of the work, especially if it is going to restrict the access into the house.

Drives that double up as the access to the front door can suggest they have two uses, for example, with a pattern of footsteps, leading you colourfully up the garden path.

TYPES OF DRIVEWAY MATERIALS

Aggregate
Loose chippings are economical, easy to lay and can be broken up with slabs to create a double strip of driveway.

Tarmac
Usually black or red, the look is very utilitarian, though black can look good with strongly architectural designs. It does tend to get mossy in gardens over time.

Concrete
Again economical, but fairly boring, though interest can be added with coloured concrete, patterns imprinted into the concrete as it's drying or adding aggregate to it. Very tough but visually unforgiving.

Block paving
Probably the most popular driveway, pavers can be made from rectangular concrete blocks or more expensive, but prettier, clay bricks or granite setts which suit period and rustic homes. The shapes create opportunity for intricate patterns but this is definitely a job for the professional.

Paving slabs
These can be laid in a random pattern over the whole drive or laid in a double strip for the car wheels only. With the former option the risk is that the front garden ends up looking a bit like a patio with a car on it, and pale paving shows up dirt and oil stains. The latter option looks good with turf or gravel chippings softening the hard area, and it's also less expensive.

Left: Wooden sleepers and flint gravel keep the look soft and natural for a beachcomber-style driveway (see page 118), with seaside colours that are easy on the eye.

Right: A rock 'n' roll theme in Leeds (see page 52) deserved glamorous materials, so crushed CD and lilac glass were perfect for the Britpop-style driveway.

Resin bond
This is a bonded surface like tarmac except the crushed stone comes in a wider range of colours and materials, such as glass, crushed CD and even computer cables. It's then 'glued' together with a transparent epoxy resin. Though a fairly uncommon material for drives, it's ideal where you want to add personality to your front garden as it allows your designs to be more flamboyant with patterns. For example, *Front of House* created a driveway for a keen salsa dancer (see left and page 14) with dance footsteps laid into the bond plus shaped patterns of green and blue glass to mimic the style of a formal garden

Adding ornaments kills two birds with one stone where there is no path to the front door and the drive doubles up as an attractive path and drive. To lay resin bond, you need a flat bonded surface beneath so it's ideal for covering up concrete and tarmac drives. Although you can buy DIY kits for small areas, this is another job for the professionals and is pricy.

PAVING AND PATHWAYS

The hard surfaces of paths and patios are easy to get wrong because they are the dominant feature that link the hard materials of the boundary to the house. They must echo at least one, or both of these, to work in style terms.

The path to your door is an essential feature of the front garden, something you'll use at least twice a day, for every day of the year. This is where the purpose of your front garden is truly crystallized – as a thoroughfare – so it must be both functional and welcoming.

DESIGNING PATHWAYS

Front garden paths should run fairly quickly to the front door, especially if you can see the door from the gate – too many curves and meanders are pointless and irritating. Widen it out near the front door or make room for a large step to create space for waiting guests and supermarket shopping. If the path crosses the front of the house, you may decide it's useful to have a hard stand for cleaning windows, or, with semi-detached houses, fast access to next door for the postman. On the other hand, this area can also be useful space for climbers, which will enhance the look of the house. If your drive doubles up as a path to the front door, as often happens where the door is on the side of the house or the driveway is in the centre, there are ways of signalling a route to the front door. Build a pattern into the material of your drive to suggest a pathway, for example, by changing the pattern of the blocks in block paving, or creating a design in resin-bonded stone. Creating a raised step out over the top of the drive around the doorway also makes the driveway-path more welcoming. If security is a worry, gravel paths crunch noisily underfoot and the sound magnifies at night, so it makes a good intruder-deterrent.

THE TECHNICAL BIT

Width

Allow enough space for two people to walk side by side, say around 800–900mm (2.6–2.9ft). Paving slabs come in standard sizes, so check your choice will fit without having to make lots of time-consuming cuts.

Foundations

Dig out a foundation beneath and fill it with compacted hardcore to about 50mm (2in). Spread a thin layer of sand and cement and lay paving on top, checking as you lay with a spirit level – then finish off by brushing dry cement in the cracks to hold the paving in place. Wait for it to go off (set) before walking on it.

Style

Paving can be laid randomly in different sizes for a rustic look, or in uniform sizes for an urban look. Riven paving and natural stone is more rustic, while flat and stippled concrete looks modern.

Edging

Gravel always needs a retaining edge – timber batten or stone – to stop it getting kicked about. Edging is useful too if the lawn is adjacent to your path because it stops grass growing up to the edge and stops you having to use edging shears after each mow. Lay edging so that it is flush with the top of the turf and the mower can pass right over the top without catching the blades.

MATERIALS FOR PAVING

Paving slabs
Paving adds instant structure. Natural stone looks good but is expensive. Concrete comes in a range of colours and looks but if you have to cut it to fit, the cut edges give the game away.

Bricks and setts
Reclaimed bricks and granite setts suit rustic themes but are prone to flaking and frost damage, though damaged bricks can be replaced. Concrete pavers have a longer life but can look municipal. The units are small and need a certain skill to lay.

Gravel
Cheap, easy to lay and good for security, gravel is often just thrown down and forgotten. Break it up with plants, boulders, sleepers or sculpture. Edge, edge, edge to keep it looking neat. Choose a colour to suit your house.

Wood
Deck can make a good path and step in front of a house provided it's not shady (and so runs the risk of becoming slippy with algae). Sleepers laid into lawns and gravel drives work well, but be prepared for hard work when shifting them around and cutting them to size.

Rubber
Recycled tyres shredded into a loose mulch are available in various colours and make a soft surface for play areas. Unlike bark, it doesn't disintegrate and need replacing every year. It can look artificial, but that might not be a problem with very architectural schemes.

Metal
Perforated metal looks good in urban schemes, though works best for small areas because it's hard to walk on in heels, gets hot in summer and it can be slippy in winter!

PATIOS

Creating a successful patio in a front garden is two parts position and one-part materials. My favourite spot for a front-garden patio is the side of the house, but gardens with privacy to the front also suit patios in the centre of the garden. I created a circular sleeper patio in the middle of a lawn for Lolly and John Holt in Manchester (left). It worked for two reasons: firstly, it integrated with the lawn because the turf ran in between the sleepers, and secondly, the privacy from the existing hedge was duplicated in a second internal screen which enclosed the patio in a semi-circle planting of bamboo. In between the planting, I set reclaimed planks at random heights with holes cut out for green Perspex, which picked up on the colour of the tiles on the house while giving the feel of enhanced privacy.

OUTDOOR SEATING AND SCREENS

Since we're talking about front gardens here, it might come as a surprise that I'm discussing sitting out at all. But why not?

So many front gardens that I've come across are just as private, and no more noisy, than the back garden. Gardens on corner plots especially are quite secluded to the side of the house, and the easy access to the back garden and the kitchen door make them perfect for converting into outdoor dining areas. All you need is to make it as private as possible and make sure that seating is secure.

When choosing where you're going to make your patio, it's best to physically choose the area for your patio rather than to design it on paper, as you will know the places you find most comfortable to sit in just by taking a chair out and trying out different spots. Bear in mind that screens don't just have to go up; you can also dig down and create sunken areas to create privacy. If the garden slopes upwards away from the house, for example, levelling off the earth will create a bank of soil behind it and enhance the seclusion. In level gardens, I love hedges for front garden privacy because they fit in everywhere and also reduce traffic noise. If you're lucky enough to already have one, optimize the density of the foliage by mulching the base with well-rotted manure or compost in winter and trim it once or twice a year to keep to size.

On *Front of House*, I designed all the patios to be oriented so seats looked back at the house rather than out onto the road. That way, the owners got to sit back and enjoy the look of the house façade, whilst the house walls combined with the screening behind conjured up a feeling of intimacy.

The trick with screening is to make it tall enough without it looking overwhelming. Though screens can be around 1.2–2m (3.9–6.6ft) tall, they're less heavy in a front-garden situation if they're see-through. Provided you can feel something physically behind you, the space feels safe and comfortable even if you're not invisible. Screens are good for making clear divisions between paths and drives, to lessen the feeling of the front garden being a thoroughfare to the front door. As for materials, there's no need to go straight for trellis. While its criss-cross pattern suits many period homes, customized screens that complement the materials on the house give you many more options. Provided you have the fence posts to support the screen, you can use all sorts of materials – perspex, glass, aluminium, stainless steel, wrought-iron, wood, bamboo, reed and even canvas. After all, the screen is not just there for privacy, it's to hammer home your style and the look of the front of your house.

Front gardens on corner plots often have room at the side of the house where it's private, usually with easy access to the kitchen door for al fresco meals

FRONT GARDEN FURNITURE

The best way to make outdoor furniture secure is to combine built-in seating and tables with easily stowable items such as folding teak chairs. Alternatively, pick furniture that looks good enough to be used indoors as well as out, like the colourful, waterproof beanbags that I used for the Edward Hopper House (see page 102).

Built-in table

Making your own built-in table is simple. For the patio at Jeanette and Colin's Diamond Italian house (see left) we concreted in four fence-posts then attached sawn-down and sanded scaffold boards to the top. Then I pinned on a beading of red rope to the outside so it harmonized with the red-rope diamonds on the front of the house.

Built-in seats

Built-in wooden seats and benches can be made, based on the same principle as the table. Another option is heavy stone-filled gabion baskets, with comfy cushions placed on top that can be brought in and out when you're using them. I used this idea for the Waterfall House in Cardiff (see above) because stone is ideal for creating a rustic, natural look.

Tree seats

Building a bench around the trunk of a tree is another attractive feature, which even if rarely used, suggests that the front garden has a function and is a sociable place. You can build tree seats from wood or hazel rods and willow, or buy fairly expensive wrought-iron seats. They all work on the same circular shape that fits around the trunk with the tree canopy overhead, meaning no-one can steal your tree seat in a hurry!

Gabion-style seating provides a wonderful view of the waterfall on the side of the house and being built in situ, is secure enough to leave outside even in a front garden.

Padlocks and chains

With free-standing furniture, secure it with a padlock and chain to a bolt in the wall or a fence-post concreted in the ground. This works well if the surface is gravel because you can hide the chain under the aggregate, or where foliage can cover the chain. An example is the Art Deco House in Leeds (see page 138), where the seats were simply chained around the tree trunks.

CASE STUDY
Screens for a Princess house

This Liverpool front garden was overgrown and unloved, just one large unkempt lawn and a path leading to the front door and a side gate. But if straggly and messy is how friends saw the garden, it's far from how the owner, Julie King, sees herself. Liking things 'just-so', she admits she can be a bit of a princess, and one who likes to party, enjoying nights out with the girls in the city. Interestingly, Oliver picked up on the princess tag, and went for materials like wrought-iron trelliswork and images of butterflies while I went for the party moniker and designed an urban garden to suit the city location and city-girl. Julie's garden had no real purpose except as access to the doorways and is set off the road along a walkway lined either side with houses, so is fairly private. The best opportunity was the fact the garden was wider than long, unusual for front gardens, meaning that it needed a strong shape to pull the garden together. I went for a figure of eight design with one larger circle comprising a lawn and a smaller circle closer to the side of the house for a gravel patio. To accentuate the shape and create privacy, I designed a serpentine screen of flexible marine ply to curve around the sides of the circle, painting them cream to marry with the paintwork on the house render. Julie is a self-confessed non-gardener so the planting had to be low-maintenance but pretty and flowery, so I went for a mixed planting of trees – a winter-flowering cherry, *Prunus subhirtella* 'Autumnalis Rosea', topiary for a princess feel and tough flowering shrubs which grow into self-sufficient mounds, such as *Viburnum tinus* and spring-flowering firethorn, pyrancantha.

GET WIRED FOR LIGHTS AND WATER FEATURES

Getting your front garden wired up with electricity widens the scope for lighting and water features, but there's so much more you can do than the classical water feature in the centre of the front garden.

You can use lights in conjunction with screens to make areas of the garden feel more private or distinct, or to light up driveways and make them safer and more welcoming at night. If it's moving water you're after, fountains add height and act like moving sculptures, adding dynamism, water music and a sense of fun. Even better, why not have both, using water and lights together? Manufacturers have made it simple, with a whole range of fountains and misters available with white and coloured lights built in to make them easy to install. After all, once you have electricity in the garden, it seems a shame not to make the most of it.

STYLES OF WATER

Ponds

These can be formal or informal, planted or unplanted, depending on the location. While an informal, natural-looking pond seems to suit both country and urban locations, very formal ponds look better in more built-up environments. You can buy either moulded plastic pond-liners or flexible butyl liners and determine your own shape. The most important aspect with liners is that they are level, otherwise it will be hard to disguise the plastic. Clear sharp stones out and line it with a 5cm (2in) layer of sharp sand to bed it in; try not to walk on the liner except in bare feet to avoid puncturing it. With flexible liners, wait till the water has gone in before cutting it to shape, as the weight of the water may pull it down more than you expect.

Rills

Great for slopes, rills are channels moving water from one part of the garden to another. Very fashionable, they can be made from pre-fabricated stainless steel or recycled RSJ girders and still look good.

Water features

Also known as pebble ponds, these are miniature gurglers, fountains and spillers that can be bought ready-made, in kit form, or customized to your own design. Because they recycle the water, they're simple, requiring only a small plastic reservoir and a source of electricity. Since they're small, make sure they're well secured to the ground for security.

Left: A rill made from a steel girder and metal flooring create a modern industrial feel.

Right: A large ceramic pot bubbling with water is self-contained and simple to make.

Far left: A mister is as easy to install as a pond pump and makes for an eerie feel for the Gothic garden (see also page 19), especially when lit up at night.

Left: In this Japanese garden (see also page 82), black pond dye reflects the styling of the house and stepping stones accentuate the oriental feel.

ACCESSORIES FOR PONDS

- **Fountains.** These have a dual function: to look attractive and to oxygenate the water, which stops stagnation and algae forming. They add height and movement to a garden, though the ultimate height of the jet depends on the power of the pump and the size of the pond. Make sure that water doesn't overshoot the side of the pond.
- **Misters.** An alternative to fountains, these take water from the pond and ionise it to make it look like smoke. This is ideal for eery night-time effects, especially as you can buy misters with built-in lights. Misters must be set into the pond at an exact height to work, so buy a float at the same time as the mister for simple installation.
- **Stepping stones.** Ideal for an oriental look and fun for the kids, stepping stones are easy to position. Just set them, with the flat side facing up, onto haunches of fast-drying cement. Make sure that two-thirds of the stone is submerged and place them one pace apart for easy crossing.
- **Water plants.** A mixture of plants suits a wilder scheme, especially if you mimic nature using floating oxygenators to keep the water sweet, along with submerged plants and marginals that live at the pond's boggy edges. For a formal planting, restrict the range of plants to one or two classic plants like water lilies or architectural water iris.
- **Pond dye.** This comes in powder form, and just a couple of teaspoons will turn a 2sq m (21.5sq ft) pond into an inky black pool. It's good for hiding the workings of pumps, stepping stones and so on in the base of the pond and is not harmful to either plant or aquatic life. It also brilliantly enhances the reflective qualities of the water, mirroring the facade of the house.

LIGHTS

Types available include:
- **Recessed deck lights.** Useful for under seats, steps, along paths or in fences and under-foot in decking.
- **Low-voltage LED lights.**
- **Spike lighters.** Useful for angling light at or up through features to graze statues, trees, fountains. I used low voltage uplighters on spikes in the Mondrian garden (see pages 115 and 136), positioning them beneath the perspex screen. That way at night, the screen is flooded with light and colour while the driveway behind fades away into darkness, making the already private front garden feel more like a back garden.

UNDERSTANDING THE ELECTRICS

You'll need a qualified electrician to connect your feature or lights, either by installing a waterproof outdoor socket or by linking the cable to the mains indoors. While electricity must be handled only by people who know what they're doing, there's a lot of work that you can do to minimize the cost of calling in the electrician. Once you decide on the source of the electrics, you can dig a trench for the cable. Ideally this will be 66cm (2ft) deep and somewhere you're unlikely to want to dig in future. For safety, use armoured cable or a low-voltage appliance with a transformer, so that neither you nor prospective owners are at risk. A residual current device (RCD, also known as circuit breaker) is also essential as if the cable is severed it will cut the current before it can give you an electric shock.

DOS AND DON'TS

DO

- Look for opportunities to complement the house in the front garden, such as the driveway and boundaries, choosing materials that accentuate those on the facade.
- Be realistic about what you can and can't do and allocate a budget for professionals to do stuff you can't. It's worth that spending extra to get a hard-wearing finish that will last.
- Work on the privacy aspect. Once you feel secluded, your options increase, whether you just fancy some seating, an area for entertaining or sunbathing or even a hot tub!
- Think carefully about where you park the car as it will affect all other options. Make scale cut-outs of your cars that fit your scale drawing to discover new places to park.
- Plan what you're going to do with evils like dustbins and recycling boxes and look for opportunities to create extra storage in features like seating or underneath decking.
- Get the hard landscaping right if you don't want to spend much time in your front garden, but do want it to look good. It will require much less maintenance than plants.
- Save some money for plants. Front gardens always look better if softened and balanced by some planting, even if it's just a few large low maintenance shrubs.

DON'T

- Shop just at the garden centre. To find materials that suit your house trawl salvage yards, the internet, stone and builder's merchants, local craft fairs and art shops. Look for ways to customise mass-market products.
- Assume that non-conformance is bad. If other gardens and houses are dull and bland, doing something different, if done to a high-standard, can only look better.
- Start planting before you finish the hard landscaping. Plants and tree roots are always the first casualties when excavations start. If you have recently planted something, the odds are you can dig it up and grow it in a pot and then replant it in its new home later.
- Think that substituting hard landscaping for lots of small ornaments or DIY features will work. Without a proper structure, the space will just look messy and confusing.
- Assume you have to get rid of existing landscape totally. You can combine it with another material and so halve your costs. Gravel, for example, can look messy if ignored, but is great edged or with another material such as slabs or sleepers incorporated into it.
- Start DIY hard landscaping without setting out the order in which the work is going to be done and timetabling the delivery of materials.
- Forget that hard landscaping should make your life easier. Incorporate materials that cut down on work, such as mowing edges to your lawn, easy steps on slopes, non-slip materials, as well as mortared paving joints and membrane under gravel for less weeding.

CHAPTER 8
SOFT
LANDSCAPING

The area in front of a house is a liberating place to garden because it's free of the pressures found in a back garden – the needs of your children, pets and so on. As a keen gardener, my front gardens have always reflected the fact that I love to grow plants and want to use every available piece of ground. Over the years, my various front gardens have been planted with everything from pretty herbaceous borders to hedges of sunflowers, collections of ornamental grasses to rows of vegetables.

But front garden plants can do more than just make up the garden. Your choice of plants can reflect the period of your house, be it Victorian or modern, or say something more personal about you. Try and choose plants that not only complement the front of your house but also strongly convey your sense of style, just as you would choose the furniture in your lounge or bedroom.

FRONT GARDENS

Before you set your heart on plants that suit your house and personality you have to know what will grow in your soil, aspect and climate.

If you're unsure, you can buy soil-tester kits from a garden centre or you can ask people who live on the same side of the road as you. Alternatively, seek advice from the knowledgeable souls at a garden centre.

The other important point is to get your plants off to a really good start when you plant them. Improve the soil before you plant by turning it over and mixing in garden compost with each forkful. This will help to feed the plants and also make them less prone to drying out in their first summer when they're still putting down roots and establishing themselves.

If you've moved into a house and have lived with the original plants for a season or two, decide whether you actually like them or not. There's no point being sentimental about them – after all, you wouldn't live with an avocado bathroom suite you hated just because it was there when you arrived. Why put up with a plant that's in the way every time you open your car door, or a flower colour that sets your teeth on edge? Get rid of it and move on. Alternatively, take advantage of the fact that small plants can be easily moved to better positions during their dormant season.

When it comes to deciding which plants to buy, don't forget to consider the functions of your choice. Some plants are really useful as screens, acting to buffer the noise from the road or to hide the downstairs windows from passers-by. Other plants are brilliant softeners; placed around the edges of steps and pathways, they can take away hard edges and make the structure of the house and garden feel part of the landscape.

Consider whether you want a tree. Because we tend to be focused on either colours or shapes, trees often don't make it onto the list. Maybe that's because people are frightened about planting trees since they think they will take ages to perform and also because they imagine that the tree may outgrow the space. But bear in mind a tree is like any other shrubby, woody plant – after two years it will really start to fill out its space and earn its place. Okay, after 12 years or so it may start to need some pruning, but you still have a decade of a plant providing privacy, cover and colour for the house and garden, and with hardly any work from you.

BEFORE YOU PLANT CHECKLIST

The work. How high maintenance do you want your garden to be? Do you feel comfortable gardening at the front?

Access. Is there easy access from where you store tools such as lawnmowers and hosepipes?

The conditions. Do you need specialist plants to cope with extreme conditions such as road pollution, poor soil or exposure to cold or winds?

Functions. Do you need plants to fulfil a function such as screening the house from the road, hiding bins, defining your boundary or disguising a manhole? Do you want plants in groups in beds or just one or two specimens?

What style? Do you want to reflect the style of planting that was popular when your house was built? This could be a Victorian fernery or colonial boxed beds with formal bedding plants. Or do you want to reflect your own style?

Your wishlist. What do you want plants to give you? Your desires could include specific colour, seasonal colour, scent, year-round foliage, fruit and berries or the ability to attract wildlife.

PLANTING FRONT GARDENS

Whenever I'm building a garden, all the hard materials of paths, drives and fences are done first, but these elements lack cohesion until the plants arrive. Foliage, whether it's grass, trees or herbaceous leaves, provides a visual buffer that takes away the hard lines and tempers sharp colours, allowing them to sit side by side. In the case of the *Front of House* that was given a modern art look, (below and page 84) the perspex screens that divided the garden from the driveway looked stunning, but it wasn't until the bamboos, verbena and large phormium were swaying around them that they looked like they'd always been there.

Most front gardens are planted by default. Things are bought and just planted in the ground. If they grow, they're left to get bigger, and if they don't, they get replaced by something that will survive. But this is missing a trick. Unlike the back garden, which is viewed mostly from the house, front garden plants should be influenced by the style of your house, either the period of the house or, in the case of many post-war homes, the personal style you're aiming for.

New Zealand flax (*Phormium tenax*) makes a bright Perspex screen look at home, softening its hard lines, casting shapely shadows, and concealing a driveway to the right.

CREATING A STYLE WITH PLANTS

Period houses

With their strong symmetry and signature architecture, all classic-fronted houses – Georgian, Edwardian or Victorian – deserve bold gardens in a modern or traditional English style. Period houses in cities tend to have very small front gardens and many suffer from a lack of front railings, which were removed in World War II. So, one way to go is to attempt a complete restoration, using pollution-tolerant evergreen shrubs such as variegated aucuba and box (*Buxus sempervirens*) – authentically stoic but pretty dreary. You could get away with something as traditional as topiary or as contemporary as a prairie meadow in your front garden provided it's contained within a structure of low box-hedges (or even timber-edged beds), which echo the neat lines of the house. You could also go tropical, but in a Victorian way – all the same plants are there, but so is the symmetry to tie the design to the front of the house. The same is true for bedding schemes, which the Victorians loved in canal beds and borders. Keep the formality of the beds, but plant more softly, adding taller plants like grasses to bring it all up to date. While the Victorians planted to show that they controlled nature, by contrast we plant to get back in touch with it.

Post-war houses

Many post-war houses have little character and not much to recommend their architecture, so how you plant the garden comes down to two main issues: your style and what you want from your plants (colour, screening, security). While designing gardens for *Front of House*, it's been clear that gardens have to function – paths have to run to doors and gates and so on – but it's in

Wispy *Verbena bonariensis* creates a delicate screen between the borders and paths. The large Chusan palm behind looks tropical but is hardy enough for our chilly climate.

the detail that you can add personality. Here are some examples of how I used plants to reflect the owner's personality:

Rock 'n' Roll garden (see page 52). Because Jason is the bass guitarist in a rock band, the house was given a glamorous circular door with bright red paintwork. I reflected the bold shape in a large geometric bed which screened the lounge window from the road and used softly screening plants with a contemporary feel. These included the black-stemmed bamboo, *Phyllostachys nigra*, spandex-yellow rudbeckia and the stripy grass, *Miscanthus sinensis* 'Zebrinus', surely the horticultural equivalent of leopardskin pants!

Celtic garden (see page 99). Dave's patriotism was reflected in the use of local Welsh plants, including many ferns, such as asplenium, dryopteris and athyrium, plus winter-stemmed dogwoods and hawthorn – the kind of plants you'd expect to see growing in the Welsh hills and valleys. These make good edging plants and were great softeners for the large driveway he needed to park two cars.

Colonial garden (see page 15). Neighbours Julia and Bernadette live next to door to each other in a semi-detached house that faces a T-junction, reminiscent of the long sweep up to colonial mansions. I chose the style that Dutch and English settlers took with them to the Americas – English formal hedged beds with a contemporary twist, filling box-edged beds with meadow-style cosmos and low grasses. The colonial-style verandah that Oliver designed for the front of house was planted up with 'Blush Noisette' roses – a brilliant climber for pergolas because it flowers all the way up the posts.

Mediterranean garden (left and page 152). Elaine de Monaco has a penchant for landscapes enjoyed on her holidays, so her house's blue and white theme was mirrored with flowers that matched the colour of the stencils, including sky-blue agapanthus and mauve verbena. The centrepiece of the garden was a Chusan palm (*Trachycarpus fortunei*), which created an exotic feel but was ideal for the Leeds climate because this hardy palm can take temperatures down to −10ºC (14ºF).

Motorbike garden (see pages 117 and 123). Eve Rowe is a motorbike fanatic with a five-year-old son who needed space out front to play on his bikes. With a long, shared driveway between two gardens, the obvious solution was to fence off one area and make it safe near the road, creating a patterned, resin-bonded driveway that served both as an attractive path to the front door and as a playground. The soil was planted up with tough plants that could take kids' play, including ground cover of rough-and-tumble elephants ears (*Bergenia cordifolia*), hardy geraniums and silver birch (*Betula utilis* var. *jacquemontii*) for white winter bark and butter-yellow autumn leaves.

Gothic garden (see page 19). Ange and Lee are committed Goths who like to walk on the dark side, loving horror movies, black clothes and their pet tarantula! Before the *Front of House* team arrived, their front garden was simply a path to the front door, so it was a blank canvas on which to create a picturesque scene, all viewed from a bench carved to look like a medieval stocks. Oliver's silver-grey house created a fitting backdrop for plants with eerily black leaves, including the black lily turf (*Ophiopogon planiscapus* 'Nigrescens'), shiny-purple autumn berries (*Callicarpa*) and the silvery foliage of evergreen cotton lavender (*Santolina*) and *Senecio* 'Sunshine'.

PLANNING BEDS AND BORDERS

Having worked out what will grow in your soil and chosen the style of the plants you want for your front garden, it's time to decide how you will position them.

The traditional way to plant is to create borders that skirt the edge of the garden, with a lawn in the middle. While this can look brilliant, you're not obliged to plant this way any more than you have to place all the furniture around the perimeter of a room. What's more, in small gardens, this creates problems because borders are thin, with insufficient space for shrubs to grow. This means you're constantly lopping back plants, which in turn spoils their natural shape and reduces the amount of flowers they produce.

This type of planting also creates a very static space. If you walk into the middle, there's nowhere to go and little opportunity for interaction with the garden. Instead, use borders to create a route around the garden.

Try swapping the traditional positions of the lawn and borders, so turf is at the edge and the plants in the middle. It creates a focal point and a route round the garden.

PLANTING STYLES

The grid

Imagine a Mondrian painting and the way the space is divided into geometric-shaped areas. They can run parallel to the house or at an angle, with some sections filled with lawn or water and others with gravel and plants. Use a material such as timber or granite paving to edge the different areas. The look is contemporary and, if all the hard materials link up, you can walk across it. Planted with bamboo and Japanese maples (*Acer palmatum*) creates an oriental look, which is why I used the grid pattern for Julia's Eastern-style house (see page 82).

Central bed

The kidney-shaped central bed was very fashionable in the late 80s/early 90s. It adds dynamism to gardens, allowing you to view planting from all sides, with taller plants in the centre, falling away to smaller flowers and edging plants. For the 21st century garden, you could create geometric squares and circles, or softer, organic shapes, such as ellipses, teardrops or flower shapes. Skirt the bed with lawn, gravel or paving to allow ease of access for tending the bed.

Ribbon planting

This contemporary style has plants that meander in a ribbon style through gravel. It makes for low maintenance too because there is no bare soil and weeds have little chance to grow.

Single specimens

This is a good solution for tiny front gardens where lots of small plants can look confusing. Think of the plant as a piece of sculpture and blow the budget on one large exotic plant such as a Chusan palm or a loquat. As the border will be small and there is only one plant to look after, there is a minimal amount of weeding, so this is a low-maintenance garden.

Crescent beds
These create a faux boundary so work well to create seating areas, provide a backdrop for water features, or disguise a parking area. Cut a crescent-shaped bed into the lawn or gravel, and if there is a patio, place it at the centre of the crescent. It makes a medium-sized garden feel bigger as the boundary is hidden and the eye drawn to a central feature.

OTHER IDEAS FOR FRONT GARDENS

Potager
Why traipse to an allotment when all you need is sun, good soil and a few packs of vegetable seeds for a vegetable garden? It doesn't have to let the neighbourhood down like a messy allotment – set out timber-edged beds, and grow the vegetables and salads in rows. Plant the edges with blackfly-deterring marigolds and nasturtiums and it'll look pretty while providing a convenient harvest.

Plant collection
Grow a collection of special plants that might not fit in with your back garden such as hardy carnivorous plants like sarracenia. You could even create a bog garden so you can grow exciting large-leaved plants from Brazil such as gunnera.

Annuals
Do something different with large annuals. Sow an eye-catching row of sunflowers as a summer screen or rows of spring-sown sweet peas for cutting and scenting the house. Pumpkin seeds can be sown direct into the ground in May and be harvested for soups and Halloween lanterns.

Spring meadow
Esteemed plantsman Christopher Lloyd has done it – made a meadow in front of his house, that is. Plant spring bulbs and meadow flowers into your lawn for a carpet of colour early in the year. If you have squirrels in the area, cover your tracks and clear all the grass of bulb debris or they'll go digging for the bulbs.

Herb garden
This is a great idea for hot and sunny front gardens and has the advantage of being close to the house. Mix rocket and basil with evergreen herbs such as thyme, rosemary and sweet bay so the patch looks good all year round.

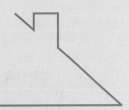

GETTING THE PROPORTIONS RIGHT
Some people can just look at a space and understand how it needs to be divided up so that the proportions look right. There's a scientific method called the Fibonacci rule, or 'golden mean', which takes its cue from the proportions seen in nature; for example, the proportion of a human head compared to the rest of the body or how the petals of a flower are arranged. If you've got a good eye, you'll be able to tell when you set your borders out whether they're too big or too small in relation to the rest of the garden. Otherwise (at the risk of being very simplistic), work on the basis that one-third planting to two-thirds garden generally looks good.

PLANTS FOR FRONT GARDENS

Some plants are better than others for front gardens because they screen, are architectural or are low maintenance.

BAMBOO

Bamboo is a great front-garden plant because it has height without being oppressive, so it screens the front windows from the road without making them dark. While not strictly evergreen, since the leaves look tatty in winter, the plants keep their structure year-round, but are much softer than many evergreen shrubs. If you've been put off bamboo because of its reputation for being invasive, don't worry. While some species do spread – sasa and pleioblastus, for example – and send out runners that sprout shoots all over the place, many are clump-forming or spread only gradually. My favourites include black-stemmed bamboo, *Phyllostachys nigra*, the stems of which start out olive-green and gradually turn shiny black. *Phyllostachys aurea* is similar with golden stems. *Fargesia nitida* is good for making hedges because it spreads slightly with thin verdigris-green culms and delicate fluttery leaves. While bamboo accentuates an oriental look, it also suits urban and contemporary themes.

ORNAMENTAL GRASSES

I like tall grasses in front gardens for the same reason I like bamboo – they are soft and screening without being claustrophobic, and look more modern than a shrubbery. My favourite is *Miscanthus sinensis* and its varieties because the flowers are pretty tassels and the foliage is less sharp than similar pampas grass. Although it dies down in winter, you can leave the foliage in place as it pales, cutting it down to ground in February before the fresh green growth appears. This way you'll only be without cover for the first few months of the year. *Calamagrostis* 'Karl Forster' is another winner, with very upright foliage and purplish flowers fading to fawn in autumn and winter. For more evergreen grasses but lower at around knee-height, try *Stipa arundinacea*, which makes curls of bronze foliage and *Stipa tenuissima*, which swishes around like blonde ponytails. There's no need to cut back stipa, just comb out the dead leaves in late winter to make way for the fresh stuff.

HARDY EXOTICS

These are plants with larger-than-life leaves that have earned the term 'architectural' because of their interesting shapes. They're the modern alternative to dumpy, shapeless shrubs that look

Far left: Black-stemmed bamboo *Phyllostachys nigra* is well-behaved and a good screening plant that sways prettily in the breeze.

Left: Ideal for screens and backdrops to flower borders, *Miscanthus sinensis* varieties vary in size and colour of leaf, including fashionable bands and zebra stripes.

Left: Phormium's lance-like leaves break up the humdrum of less shapely shrubs, and make an ordinary garden feel more exotic

Centre: Use Alchemilla's prettily scalloped leaves and lime-green sprays of summer flowers for flouncy ground cover around steps and pathways.

Right: Allium and roses mix bold shapes with softer ones to hammer home a strong colour scheme.

the same all year round. I like them, but because of their durability, many are used in municipal schemes, so you need to be imaginative when planting them. You could, for example, go for soft, wispy flowers like *Verbena bonariensis* or a ground cover of clematis. For arching, 2.4-m (8-ft) leaves, *Phormium tenax* comes in olive-green or purple and grows in sun or shade. When mature, it flowers with big spikes of white blooms. The cookianum varieties have more interesting stripy and colourful leaves, but they don't get too big and are good for pots. Phormium looks similar to cordyline when at the garden centre, but cordyline (especially the purple-leaved variety) is less hardy and ultimately grows big enough to have a trunk. It flowers when mature and is gloriously scented. *Fatsia japonica* has shiny, evergreen leaves and produces creamy, globular flowers late in the year. It looks good backing on to the house as a wall shrub. Yucca succeeds in a well-drained sunny spot, but the sharp leaves need careful positioning if you have children and pets. *Yucca filamentosa* is less lethal than *Y. gloriosa* – it's not called Spanish dagger for nothing.

GROUND COVER

Evergreen ground cover is superb for anchoring the hard landscaping of the garden, and making features look more established. My favourites include bergenia, with its large, oval foliage and spikes of white or bright-pink flowers in late winter. Plant it around steps and the edges of decking. Heuchera is great – especially the purple types – because they make a good colour break next to the green of herbaceous leaves; they're happy in sun or shade, and slugs don't bother them. Use it to hide the edges of pebble ponds, pergola posts and around the base of seats. *Alchemilla mollis* is another plant I use

a lot – with scalloped, apple-green leaves and foamy, lime-green summer flowers. It seeds around in sun or shade and creates a skirt for other taller plants. It will even grow in between paving and gravel gardens where it's hot and dry.

FLOWERS

Choose flowers on the basis of what will grow in your garden and will suit the colour and style of your house, then plant confidently. One plant won't make enough of a splash; you have to plant in groups for impact. If there's room, repeat the groups around the garden to create the illusion of being surrounded by flowers. If you go for a colour scheme, lots of small, fuzzy flowers will shout louder if they're backed up with the same colour in a bold shape, such as a hybrid clematis, peony, allium or red hot poker. If you plant in groups of three or five, with flowers that bloom in each season, there will always be lots of flowers, even if it's the same plants right across your garden. For example – if you wanted a pinky-purple look right through the year, you could run from winter crocus, to anemone blanda, then tulips, alliums, to summer roses, followed by penstemon, sedum and finally late-autumn asters.

DESIGNING THE MODERN LAWN

Grass is a brilliant ground cover and is about as straightforward as plants can get. Even an ordinary rectangular lawn gives a garden instant clarity and structure when it's freshly mown and edged.

Edged with planed timber and dissected with formal gravel paths, artificial turf could fool a groundsman and makes a pleasing surface for a putting green in the English with a Twist garden.

Unfortunately, its hard-working nature and ability to cope with neglect means the potential of lawns is often overlooked. We've become accustomed to seeing them overgrown and creeping into borders. But turf can look fun, offering great opportunities to create pictures and shapes. You can cut it to any pattern and mix it with other materials, so why not see where your imagination takes you, whether it's a turf maze or your house number emblazoned in emerald-green blades.

HOW TO MAKE PATTERNS

When making patterns with turf it's important to have a good quality sward, so if yours is filled with daisies and dandelions, consider lifting it and laying fresh stuff. Don't try to lay the turf into the shape of your pattern like a jigsaw, as this will probably produce lots of small edges that are likely to dry out and die. Instead, lay the turf beyond the area of your intended pattern, allow it to grow and then cut it to shape. The best tool for cutting turf neatly is a bread knife. Draw your pattern on to the turf with white ground-marking paint (this will get cut off as the grass grows). For straight edges, use taut string held on bamboo pegs; for curves, use a hosepipe. For repeated curves of the same shape, make a template out of a piece of marine ply.

For the turf to keep its shape and look strong, ideally it needs to be edged with a hard material.

Choose one that blends with the rest of the garden and the house such as bricks or granite setts; timber pegged into the ground or stainless steel or aluminium also work well. Make sure the level of your edging is no higher than the turf so the blades of the lawnmower don't get caught.

Ideas for turf patterns
- Mazes
- House names and numbers
- Chequerboard, stripes and swirls
- Football team emblems
- Yin-yang
- Flags and patriotic symbols
- Letters, initials and names
- Teardrops and leaf shapes

TURF ALTERNATIVES

If you don't want to mow, but don't want the surface of your front garden covered with paving or gravel, there are many alternatives. The latest artificial turf looks incredibly realistic even from just a few feet away and comes in a range of shades and lengths of sward. It's ideal for a front garden that you don't regularly walk on, where grass is more of a visual feature. The key to making it look realistic is in the laying. Professionals will do this for you, but if you do it yourself, concentrate on making sure the turf is level and put in a mowing edge to hide the unrealistic corners.

Stonecrop (*Sedum*) species

This is another interesting evergreen alternative. The most convenient way to buy stonecrop is a ready-made matting, which can be unrolled and cut to shape just like turf. The effect of the red and green colours of these succulent plants is of a rich tapestry. They're very drought-tolerant, so ideal for south-facing, sloping front gardens. They also come into their own as green roofing, on top of porches, sheds and between paving stones or even the central strip of a driveway.

Chamomile

The pineapple-scented foliage of chamomile has long been used as a mowing-free alternative to lawns, but it can't take much trampling, so is ideal for front gardens. The variety 'Treneague' is the best for lawns because it's non-flowering. It's very expensive, however, because you have to buy each of the pots individually and plant closely, so is better for small areas. Brush horticultural grit underneath the plants to help reduce weeding and to set off the foliage.

MOUNDED AND UNDULATING LAWNS

Green mounds in lawns are a quirky feature, adding a mysterious look in the tradition of the garden knoll or burial mounds. Though their roots are ancient, their geometry is modern, making a natural focus and suiting all styles of garden. If you have a large area of lawn in your front garden, a mounded shape is a modern alternative to a specimen tree in the middle or installing a water fountain.

To create the height of the mound, you'll need to buy topsoil and the cheapest way to do this is by the cubic yard. The best way to make the shape is by stacking up the soil and then using a plasterer's float to mould it and firm it down.

FRONT GARDEN LAWNS...

...rarely get used, so why not buy top-quality turf and go for a bowling green look that will turn the neighbours green with envy.

...are the best place to plant through the lawn with brightly coloured spring bulbs such as crocus. *Crocus tommasinianus* is the best species for naturalizing, as the corms will colonize underground and over the years create a carpet of late-winter colour.

...look even better with a sprinkle of lawn fertiliser in spring and autumn. Spring fertiliser feeds the grass, providing leaf-making nitrogen for lots of lush, green growth. Autumn feeds focus on the roots and promote the health of the plants.

...should never be shapeless. Geometry is always a way of creating a neat, designed look. Don't think of the shape of your borders first; think of the shape of the lawns – grass always stands out more than soil.

...should be circular or oval if you want to make a long, thin space appear bigger, or linear if you want a formal look which leads the eye to a focal point, so don't have it pointing to the gasworks! Curvy lawns should have long, graceful sweeps, not like an amoeba with arbitrary ins and outs. If you have a good eye, experiment with a ground-making spray or, for a more scientific method, with a peg and taut line.

CASE STUDY
An Art Deco lawn

The *Front of House* team paid a visit to a period house in Leeds that was in need of restoration and a replacement for the sea of gravel out front. The aim of the garden design was to complement the Art Deco style of the house and took its cue from the curved prow shape of the building. The focus of the garden is a central elliptical border dotted with flame-shaped cypress trees and flanked on three sides by lawn (see also page 138). Either side of the bed, the lawn is elongated with a scalloped edge to give the appearance of curtains or an Art Deco mirror, while accentuating the flowerbed. The top section is cut into a chequerboard of paving and turf. The style of the garden hints at the theatrical nature of Art Deco, while echoing the look of the furniture of the period.

And there's plenty of the owner, Kay Kirkby's, personality too. The blue footsteps running up the resin-bonded driveway suggests a path to the front door while reflecting her love of salsa dancing, and her aromatherapy work is referenced in a planting scheme of shrubs for essential oils, such as rosemary, lavender and artemisia.

A QUICK GUIDE TO TURFING

Buying. Turf is sold in rolls and is available in either expensive, high-quality grade (for a bowling-green look) or utility (more suitable for regular trampling). You can lay it all year round provided you water it in dry weather. Order it in advance and get it delivered no more than a day or two before you will lay it as rolled-up grass quickly goes yellow.

Laying. Preparation is key, so clear the ground of stones and rake it level before you start laying turf, firming the soil with your feet. Start at a straight edge such as a path, then lay turves flush with each other with the joints staggered like brickwork. Work off a plank to spread your weight and avoid damaging the grass.

Aftercare. Avoid walking on it for a week of two after laying and water the lawn if it doesn't rain within a week. Give the grass its first mow after a couple of weeks with the lawnmower blades on the highest setting.

HEDGES AND SCREENS

One of the quickest ways to make the front of your house look more natural and private, without making yourself lots of work, is by planting a hedge.

That wall of green is the perfect antidote to the hard effect of bricks, pavements, street lamps and brightly coloured cars. It's also far more economical than walling or fencing and if privacy is your aim, you can get away with a far taller hedge than fence, without it looking overwhelming. A hedge also can filter pollution and noise, whilst providing cover and food for wildlife.

What puts many homeowners off is the overwhelming choice of hedging plants and the idea that trimming hedges means lots of work. But it doesn't have to be this way…

CHOOSING HEDGING PLANTS

Everyone wants the perfect hedge – evergreen, low-maintenance and good-looking – but the truth is, all hedges have their pros and cons and it's about picking the hedge that suits you and your site best. Bear in mind that while evergreen hedges keep their leaves through winter, they lack the dynamism of deciduous hedges, which change with the seasons. Regardless of whether they keep their leaves or not, all hedges keep their structure throughout the year. If you want privacy just in the summer, you might gain even more from choosing a deciduous hedge; hawthorn, for example, provides spring scent and beech offers autumn colour.

TOP FIVE FRONT GARDEN HEDGES

Beech (*Fagus sylvatica*)
Deciduous, but beech hedges hold on to copper autumn foliage through much of winter, dropping it just before the emergence of silky green leaves in late spring. Suits rustic and city locations and grows at a medium rate. Very similar to hornbeam (*Carpinus betulus*) but the leaf colour is richer. Mixes well with yew for a tweedy tapestry effect in autumn. Trim once in August. Best in larger gardens.
Minimum height: 1.2m (4ft)

Yew (*Taxus baccata*)
This classic evergreen conifer and topiary plant is ideal for introducing quirky shapes and personality. Has an undeserved reputation for being slow growing and sombre. Berries are poisonous. Very formal look; great for city gardens and for shade. Trim once in late summer and again in autumn.
Minimum height: 1.2m (4ft)

Privet (*Ligustrum*)
Golden, green or variegated evergreen leaves and a smattering of white spring flowers that are more sweetly scented than showy. It's fast growing and a real survivor, so is frequently let down by being neglected. Trim it two to three times in summer and autumn; don't let it sprawl out to take over the garden. Keep its width to no more half a metre (1.6ft). If managed well, is good for small gardens.
Minimum height: 1.5m (5ft)

Easy to grow and forgiving of neglect, the common or garden privet hedge can look neat and classy if trimmed twice a year and kept in its place.

Hawthorn (*Cratageus*)

Thorny stems and deciduous leaves and white flowers scented of bakewell tart in spring, followed by red berries in autumn. Classic country lane hedge. Trim once in summer and again in autumn. Good for small gardens if kept in check. Minimum height: 1.5m (5ft)

Viburnum tinus

Shaggy evergreen hedge with pinky-white clusters of flowers from November through to March. Trim after flowering to avoid losing too many of next winter's flowers. It's romantic in style, suitable for urban or rustic, and ideal for larger boundaries where it's allowed to mound and billow. Minimum height: 1.5m (5ft)

STARTING OFF A HEDGE

Planting a hedge is an autumn-winter job because the best-priced hedging plants are sold in bundles of bare-rooted plants rather than containers. Provided you don't plant when the ground is frozen, plants will also establish more quickly than in summer thanks to the cooler conditions and higher rainfall.

Rather than plant individually, the quickest way is to dig a trench along the intended line of your hedge, forking the base to loosen the soil and turning in some soil improver – well-rotted manure will feed and help retain moisture around the roots the following summer. Plant about 46cm (18in) apart, back-filling the soil in between the roots and firming in well with the ball of your foot. Make sure the plants go in no deeper than the soil line on the trunk.

In the first summer, give the roots a really good soak. If you're not sure whether you've watered enough, dig down with a trowel to see if the soil is dry next to the roots. Don't be too quick to shape the young plants into a hedge, just clip the sides lightly in the autumn of the following year, leaving the top growth alone. Decide on the maximum height you want the hedge to be and once it reaches just below that, give the top a trim. This stops the trunks becoming thick at the top, where you want easily sheared, bushy growth.

QUICK TIPS FOR MAINTAINING HEDGES

How to shape

Cut your hedge so it's slightly wider at the bottom than at the top to allow the light in and to stop it going brown at the base. Achieving this probably means being unnaturally brutal with the top half of your hedge; if the top half looks a bit beaten and brown, it'll quickly grow back, especially if you water and apply an annual feed of balanced fertiliser in spring.

When to cut

The time for this is late summer/early autumn as the plants aren't in full growth; like us, they prefer to relax in the heat. It also avoids disturbing birds during nesting time and gives plants time to bush out with a fresh coat of green leaves for winter. To neaten up the plants for summer, you can give them a quick trim in May after the frosts finish.

A moongate hedge, such as this pyracantha moongate, allows for glimpses of what's beyond and looks like a living sculpture.

Busy roads

If your front garden is adjacent to a very busy road, avoid conifers such as yew, leyland and lawson cypress. Being evergreen, they're susceptible to poisoning by pollution (making the leaves go brown) and if roads are salted in winter, the spray from passing cars turns the foliage black. Thorny plants like holly and hawthorn are not a good idea either because the spiny stems and leaves hook any litter blowing down your street. Better choices for these situations include privet, beech and *Lonicera nitida*.

Best tools

Cordless hedge-trimmers are great for the average front garden, where cutting time takes around 30–40 minutes, because you don't have to worry about cutting through the electric cable. With mains-powered trimmers, use a plug-in circuit breaker (RCD), which instantly cuts the electricity supply and keeps you safe should you trim through the cable.

HEDGES WITH PERSONALITY

Not all hedges have to be square! Because of their tolerance of trimming, hedging plants offer a great opportunity for you to create interesting shapes.

Moongates

A moongate is a circular window that allows enticing glimpses of what's beyond. You can create one in an existing hedge or grow a young hedge into a moongate by manipulating the main stems into shape. Ideally, make a frame to train the stems around, then prune the smaller stems to clear the view. Don't just cut out a hole or you'll lose the top of the hedge.

Straight edges and wavy tops

To get a really straight top to your hedge for a formal look, make a simple wooden frame by securing two lengths of timber batten at either end of the hedge and then tying a length of string between them at the height you want the cut. Use a spirit level to get the string level and then cut to this line. Alternatively, for something a bit different and more sweeping, or to echo the contours of the surroundings, cut the top into serpentine waves. This is trickier as you can't use a line. Instead, use ground-marking paint to mark where you want your cuts to be and follow the contours. Aim for gentle S-shaped undulations, with each peak and trough stretching over at least a couple of metres (6½ft).

Mixing varieties

For an unusual textural effect, try mixing different shades of conifer hedging with beech. Good mixers include dark-green yew (*Taxus baccata*) mixed with golden yew (*T.b* 'Aurea'), or copper beech (*Fagus sylvatica* 'Purpurea Group') with the ordinary green beech (*Fagus sylvatica*) or golden with green privet. When planting, alternate the plants to create a stripy look, create a couple of bands either side of a gate, or jumble them up to create a tapestry.

Planting with climbers

Turn your hedge into a support for lightweight climbers such as red-hot *Eccremerocarpus scaber* and climbing nasturtium. Tough honeysuckles can cope right in the base of conifer hedges where they can hide brown, dead areas along the bottom.

CLIMBERS

Climbers inhabit vertical space and are brilliant for softening and hiding hard features – perfect for the front of your house.

Left: Boston ivy wallpapers house façades with ivy-like leaves which turn flaming red before dropping in autumn and is less damaging to bricks and mortar than true ivy.

Right: Wisteria needs a strong support for its heavenly-scented early spring flowers away from east winds and late frosts which can decimate buds and flowers.

A safe way to transform the façade of a building, climbers never look out of place and grow to give the place an established look. Of course, different plants have strong associations with styles and definitely impart a flavour: porches twined with roses and clematis always say 'cottagey', while passion flowers with their waxy flowers and orange fruit suggest something more exotic.

There are different looks you can get from climbers. Only a few plants will smother the whole of the house – ivies, Boston ivies, Virginia creepers and climbing hydrangea (but very slowly). If your house is semi-detached you should think carefully before planting one of these because you're also deciding how your neighbour's house will look and there is the maintenance of having to cut back mature climbers from guttering and windows.

For a blanket of summer flowers, you can't beat roses, but they need pruning and training every winter, tying in the stems and cutting back the shoots for that clad look. When choosing, be aware that some flower in June and July, then stop, while others flower continuously but in less abundance. Wisteria can also be trained for bands of gorgeously scented, pendulous lilac flowers in May, but you need space (a good 8m/26ft of frontage) and a strong framework for those woody, twining stems.

For plants that frame doorways and porches, roses, winter-flowering *Clematis cirrhosa* and *Solanum jasminoides* 'Album' (south-facing, sheltered sites) are ideal. All clematis tend to scramble up then sit like basking cats on top of structures, so are good for growing over the top of garages, porches and sheds.

STARTING OFF A CLIMBER

1 Before you plant twiners and wall plants, stretch galvanized or plastic-coated wires horizontally across the house wall at 46cm (18in) intervals. Hold them in place with vine eyes and, for really taut wires, use bolt tensioners. Self-clingers like ivies and creepers don't need wires as they stick straight on to the wall.

2 Dig a large hole 46cm (18in) out from the base of the wall, removing any rubble and replacing with fresh topsoil and garden compost to aid moisture-retention in the summer.

3 Plant the climber in the hole, tilting the plant slightly towards the support to encourage the climber on to it. With ivy and creepers, cut back the top growth to 20cm (6in) to encourage fresh new growth to stick to the wall. With twiners and wall plants, gently tie the stems on to the bottom wires.

4 Water regularly in the first year or two – the bases of house walls are very dry due to the proximity of foundations and because rain often doesn't reach there. Occasionally tie in stems to encourage them to climb.

TEN BEST CLIMBERS AND WALL PLANTS

Boston ivy (*Parthenocissus tricuspidata*)

The classic self-clinging climber for a wallpapered look from spring to autumn, with leaves that overlap like roofing tiles plus dramatic, fiery. autumn-tinted leaves. The similar Virginia creeper (*P. quinquefolia*) has five-fingered foliage with a more textured look. Less damaging to walls and mortar than ivy. Both grow to 12m (40ft) or more.

Wisteria (*Wisteria floribunda/W. sinensis*)

The pale blue spring flowers are stunning for cream-rendered houses. Fast growing but needs annual pruning for flowers. No good for gardens in cold pockets as blooms are ruined by late frosts. Will easily cover 4.6–9m (15–30ft) of frontage.

Passion fruit (*Passiflora caerula*)

Exotic June flowers followed by oval orange fruits in late summer. A soft-twining climber good for a Spanish-colonial look. Needs pruning in spring to rejuvenate. Grows to 6m (20ft) or so.

Roses

The quintessential cottage plants for a traditional English look and summer scent. The best choice if you want pink or cream flowers. Good varieties include the vigorous, creamy-coloured 'Madame Alfred Carriere', which grows to 6m (20ft) (and is good for shade) or small apricot 'Buff Beauty' for around doorways and porches. The June-flowering 'Blarii No2' has old-fashioned pink, scented flowers, good for combining with a late *Clematis viticella* for summer-long flowers. Pale pink 'New Dawn' is a classic for shade.

Californian lilac (*Ceanothus* 'Puget Blue')

A dark-leaved evergreen wall plant with blue spring flowers. Best on sunny walls where it will make 3.7m (12ft) in three years, though they're short-lived and often die for no reason after 12 years. Without pruning they turn into a small tree, reaching 4.6–6m (15–20ft).

Clematis armandii

A very modern, architectural evergreen climber used increasingly despite its slight frost-tenderness due to our mild winters. Fast-growing, with tropical-looking, glossy-green leaves and creamy-white scented flowers in late winter. One for a sheltered spot in sun or shade. Grows to a skinny 6m (20ft).

Grapevines

A sunny front of house is ideal for an edible grapevine. If you just want that classic Greek cover, an ornamental type such as 'Brandt' is best, with silvery summer leaves, turning scarlet before they drop in autumn. Grows to 6m (20ft).

Solanum jasminoides 'Album'

A jasmine look-alike with larger, unscented white flowers from high summer to late autumn. The look is classic country house. Suits south-facing homes with porches or extended eaves where the flowers can perch. Grows to 4.6–7.6m (15–25ft).

Japanese quince (*Chaenomeles*)

Ideal for training under north-facing windows and around porches where the March flowers and autumn fruit are reminiscent of medieval tapestries. Grows to 2.4–3.7m (8–12ft).

Jasmine (*Jasminum officinale*)

Not ideal for cladding front walls but good for tall walls, porches or garages in sun and around entertaining areas where the tremendous scent can collect, more thickly at night. Mounds into the size of a small haystack, 4.6m (15ft) or more.

PLANTING IN CONTAINERS

There is a huge choice of containers in every shape, style and imaginable material, with a vast range of plants that will grow in them.

Containers look good next to hard structures like doors, paths and gates, and provide a great opportunity to do something unique in your front garden. Because of the temporary nature of the planting, they're fun too. You can really get creative, modifying the style to suit the season.

Choose the look, shape and material of the container, then plant it up to complement the style of your home. Where you put your pots provides scope for playing with the look and perspective of your house front too. Containers can emphasize or detract from the symmetry of your house, by placing one either side of the front door for classic styles or going assymetrical for a more modern look. To make watering less of a problem, you can always hook containers up to automatic irrigation systems and timers attached to your outside tap. They cost only around £30 and can be set to come on at various times during the day to keep your plants looking tip-top.

Pots are also a good solution for soil-less front gardens, providing the opportunity to add green. If you want big plants like climbers to grow up the house, buy pots that can hold a large volume of soil, such as wooden half-barrels. Climbers won't reach the size they would if planted in the ground and will need to be regularly watered and fed monthly with a fertiliser in the growing season.

Don't forget to put heavy pebbles in the pots to weigh them down and make them harder to steal, or thread a T-bar through the drainage hole and concrete the chain into the ground beneath the pot.

CONTAINER PLANTING STYLES

Flowery effusion

A chocolate-box cottage style can only be achieved with summer bedding like traditional pelargoniums, petunias and trailing ivies and helichrysum. Good for window boxes and baskets because of the trailing aspect, but they are a lot of work, needing daily watering and weekly feeding with a high-potash fertiliser through summer. It's worth the work, as they flower from early summer till the first frosts, when they need replacing with winter bedding.

Rhythmic repetition

The repeated use of the same plant in a window box or three pots of the same shape and style. This works best with flowers that have a strong graphic shape – such as Cape daisies – or foliage, such as small grasses like stipa.

Architectural formality

Includes topiary box, bay, cypresses, pyramids and lollipops, plus more quirky shapes that can be bought ready-made at a price. Suits traditional and modern homes provided the style is formal. For a modern look, use elongated, geometrical stainless steel planters.

Exotic

Spiky shapes such as cordyline, dwarf New Zealand flax (*Phormium cookinum*), *Yucca gloriosa* and *Y. filamentosa*. Suits Mediterranean, Far Eastern, colonial and modern schemes.

Minimalist

Where the pot takes higher profile than the plant, it could just be a few coloured twigs sticking out the top or even unplanted. A good look with ali baba-style urns.

CONTAINER CHOICE

Stone. The choice for classic formal gardens, most often seen shaped as urns with swag-style decorations. Ideal for front gardens because of its heavy weight, and suits homes with pastiche pillars and porticos.

Clay. Good for Mediterranean, cottage, and formal and informal schemes in all shapes and sizes – the classic pot material, but susceptible to frost and mechanical damage unless you pay a high price tag.

Glazed. Less porous than clay and available in a wide range of colours and motifs to match paint schemes and styles, especially oriental themes. But susceptible to frost in winter and mechanical damage.

Resin and plastic. Usually made to mimic clay or stone, modern look-alikes are very convincing. Cost benefits are reaped only with larger pots, which are far cheaper than the real thing at the same size. The best choice as a clay alternative in frost-prone areas where clay tends to crack and shear, or near boisterous children and pets. Good for window boxes as weighs far less than the real thing.

Metal. Suits all styles depending on the style of home. Geometric shapes and interlocking boxes suit urban styles, but they're best for shade as roots can get too hot in sun-baked metal.

Wood. Good for rustic styles and practical as wood holds moisture better than porous clay and stone, hence good for window boxes and porches.

Rubber. An unusual material suitable for modern styles, with good moisture-retention and a strong look that suits graphic flower shapes such as daisies.

Baskets. Can be made from wire, plastic-coated or stainless steel, wicker-like plant materials and coir. For a more modern look, wicker-style cone shapes are good, especially as the plastic lining means they dry out less quickly than the traditional wire types, which you line with moss, so they suit modern lifestyles.

A single colour of **Darwin tulip** in a cubic stainless steel container has the fresh crispness of a spring vase and would look very contemporary in an urban garden.

CASE STUDY
Mediterranean containers

On our visit to Elaine de Monaco's house, we were faced with a very dreary house and an old metal porch with little character. The garden itself was a boxy square of neglected turf and a privet hedge that had been allowed to become so overgrown that it took up half the garden. This was very far from what Elaine had in mind – she was longing for some Mediterranean style to remind her of foreign holidays, complete with palms, scent and water features.

To perk up the porch and soften the concrete house, Oliver designed a series of stacked troughs to be built around an existing porch and the front doorframe. Built from timber, the boxes are lined with butyl to protect the metalwork of the existing porch, and drainage holes were made in the base of the liner and wood to allow the compost to drain. The way

the timber was screwed together matched the woodwork on the fence so the house and the garden hung together really well. Similarly, the boxes were stained with a dark oak woodstain to match the front fence and gate. To tie the porch in with the rest of the house, more boxes were made for an ungainly extension to the left of the house. These were planted with larger exotic yucca plants – great spiky shapes for attracting attention, and drought-tolerant so ideal for high-flung places where they have to survive on rainfall.

Finally, for the porch boxes I chose scented seasonal bedding flowers, including trailing plectranthus, lavender and ivy, creating a wonderfully scented welcome for owner and guests alike. Spiky leaves are also well out of the way of jabbing guests and the postman too!

DOS AND DON'TS

DO
- Be imaginative when choosing plants. Pick them to suit the soil and conditions and to emphasize your look or theme.
- Give plants a good start by digging big holes for their roots, enriching the hole with organic matter and watering plants well in the first summer. This will make it grow better and mean they're less trouble to look after long term.
- Trim your hedge, or pay someone else to do it for you, once or twice a year in late summer. Then give it a nutritious mulch in late winter to keep it dense and healthy, and create a noise-buffer between you and the road.
- Secure containers by weighing them down with heavy stones or securing them with a t-bar threaded through the drainage hole and chained into the ground.
- Place plants so they add to your privacy. Plant trees so that they grow to give shelter to your seating area or front room. Use them along paths and boundaries to mark the route, soften the edges and make the hard materials look less harsh.
- Train climbers on walls and fences to encourage them to grow over the façade. Soil near walls will be drier and often needs exchanging from builder's rubble to proper soil.

DON'T
- Keep plants that you don't like because they were there when you bought the house or for sentimental value. Replace them with something that appeals to you.
- Assume you have to spread your budget over lots of small plants. Blowing the lot on one well-shaped, mature plant can have as much impact as a sculpture.
- Let lawns get out of bounds. Create a hard edge so the lawn has a neat, crisp edge all year round. An overgrown lawn creeping into borders does nothing for any front garden.
- Plump for borders that run round the edge unless you're sure it's the best look. Central borders add shape and focus and make for interesting routes around the garden.
- Plant one of everything in the hope that something will always be in flower. In small spaces restrict the palette of plants for a strong look. Buy one of each shrub or tree and more of herbaceous plants. Plant in blocks of three or five, repeated across the garden.
- Be shy: ask for local knowledge from neighbours and at the nearest garden centre. They'll know what will grow well in your area.
- Buy plants and leave them outside the back door to be planted. Get them in the ground somewhere where the roots will stay moist, even if it's not the best place, and move them later, otherwise they'll die or not do so well once they finally get planted.

RESOURCES

GOVERNING BODIES OR ADVISORS

Federation of Master Builders (FMB)
020 7242 7583 / www.fmb.org.uk

The Guild of Master Craftsmen
01273 478449 / www.thegmcgroup.com

**NICEIC (National Inspection Council
for Electrical Installation Contracting)**
020 7564 2323 / www.niceic.org.uk

The Institute of Plumbing
01708 472791 / www.iphe.org.uk

Royal Institute of British Architects
020 7580 5533 / www.riba.org

Institute of Structural Engineers
020 7235 4535 / www.istructe.org.uk

The Royal Institution of Chartered Surveyors
0870 3331600 / www.rics.org

Landscape Architects –The Landscape Institute
020 7299 4500 / www.l-i.org.uk

Master Locksmiths Association
01327 262255 / www.locksmiths.co.uk

The Building Centre
09065 161136 / www.buildingcentre.co.uk

The Building Centre Bookshop
020 7692 4040

**Free Government Planning
Permission Guide booklet**
0870 1226 236

STOCKISTS AND SUPPLIERS

denotes environmentally friendly products and suppliers

GENERAL
Travis Perkins
01604 752424 / www.travisperkins.co.uk

Homebase
0845 077 8888 / www.homebase.co.uk

DOORS, PORCHES & ENTRANCES

Architectural Salvage
www.salvo.co.uk (recycled doors)

Magnet
01325 469441

LeeWay
0121 666 6369 (UPVC columns)

Door Furniture

A & H Brass
020 7402 1854

FSB Ironmongery
020 7255 9309

Locks Direct
0800 5421244 / www.locksdirect.co.uk

Locks on Line
0845 2300201

Vieler International Ltd
01753 866500

WINDOWS

Crittal Windows
01376 324106 / www.crittall-windows.co.uk

Glaverbel UK Ltd
01788 535353 / www.glaverbel.com
(insulated glazing)

Industrial Reclamations
01580 766395 (recycled glass bottles)

Pilkington
01744 28882 / www.pilkington.com

Stained Glass
020 88748822 / www.stainedglassguild.co.uk

The Green Bottle Unit
020 72493394 (recycled glass tiles and bricks)

Window Coverings

John Lewis fabrics department
08456 049049 (curtain fabrics)

Leeway
0121 666 7203 (shutters)

Metamark (UK) Ltd
01483 571111 (vinyl window coverings)

Red Signs
020 7739 0077 (printed blinds/sign maker)

Spectrum Blind Company
01656 723380 (venetian blinds)

Window boxes

Foxes Boxes
020 7987 0819

CLADDING AND WALL TREATMENTS

☾ Claytec Earth Bricks
020 7450 2211 (cob earth bricks)

☾ Eco Décor Ltd
01925 658295 (recycled wallpaper)

GKD
01977 686410 (metal architectural mesh)

Good Directions
02920 598118 (Chemical Solutions for copper patination)

Island Stone
0800 0839351 / www.islandstone.co.uk (stone cladding)

☾ J & J Sharpe
01805 603587 (lime render)

Metal Goods Ltd
01656 647755 (copper sheeting)

Perspex Distribution Centre
01245 232800 (perspex)

Prelasti by Pirelli
01248 421955 (rubber cladding)

Screw-fix
0500 414141 / www.screwfix.com (screws and fittings)

Shaws of Darwen
01254 775111 (tiles)

Topps Tiles
0800 783 6262 (mosaics & tiles)

Wood

Eternit
01763 264600 (weatherboard cladding)

Greenfingers
0845 3450728 / www.greenfingers.com (willow fencing)

☾ Medite ZF / Medite of Europe Ltd
01702 619044 (formaldehyde-free MDF)

☾ Salvo
01668 216494 (reclaimed stone, bricks and floorboards)

☾ The Woodshed
020 7278 7172 (reclaimed floorboards)

☾ Treework Services Ltd. Bristol, Avon
01275 464466 (timber)

Witney Sawmills, Herefordshire
01497 831656 (timber)

Paints and stains

☾ Auro Paints Ltd
01799 584888 (gloss paint)

☾ Construction Resources
020 7450 2211

☾ Green Paints
01246 432193

☾ Nature Maid Company
01952 883288 (varnish)

☾ Nutshell Natural Paints
01364 642892 (enamel paints and varnishes)

☾ Potmolen Paints
01985 213960

Decoration

Stencil Library
01661 844844 (stencils)

Butchers Plasterworks
020 7722 9771 (plaster mouldings)

Rope – Foot Rope Knots
01473 690090

LIGHTING

Eclipse Garden Lighting
01303 237273 / www.eclipse-garden-lighting.co.uk

Extremis
01483 877875

Mathmos
020 7549 2700

Tom Dixon
020 7792 5335 (Jack lights)

Arthur Beale
020 7836 9034 (sailing lanterns)

Metalarte
www.metalarte.com

Deltalight (UK) Ltd
01428 651919

CP Sound
01784 461614 (neon lighting)

Silvernutmeg
01254 820478 (fire pit)

PONDS, ELECTRICS AND WATERING EQUIPMENT

Aegean Spas
020 8959 1529 / www.aegeanspas.co.uk

CEF
01603 761350 / www.cef.co.uk

Hozelock
0118 940 3785 / www.hozelock.com

Oase
www.oase-uk.com

Water Gardening Direct
01778 341199 / www.watergardeningdirect.com

PAVING, ARTIFICIAL TURF, MULCH

Borderstone
01938 570410 / www.borderstone.co.uk

Bradstones
01335 372289 / www.bradstones.co.uk

CED Ltd
01708 867237 / www.ced.ltd.uk

Derbyshire Aggregates
01629 636500 / www.derbyshireaggregates.com

Evergreens
01572 768208 / www.evergreensuk.com

Sureset
01985 841180 / www.sureset.co.uk

Verde Sports
01254 831666 / www.verdesports.com

WunderMulch
01933 625773 / www.wundermulch.co.uk

METAL FLOORING

Aalco
01932 250100 / www.aalco.co.uk

Rycon Steels
02920 498511 / www.ryconsteels.co.uk

FENCING AND DECKING ETC

Cannock Gates
08707 541813 / www.cannockgates.co.uk

Keyline
www.keyline.co.uk

Railway Sleepers
www.justsleepers.com

RMC
www.readymix.co.uk and www.stone4home.com

Rowlinsons
01270 506900

Tropical Surrounds
01264 773006

Uniglaze
01603 484494 / www.uniglaze2.co.uk

FURNITURE AND POTS

Adirondack Outdoors
01252 692513

Apta Pottery
01233 621090 / www.apta.co.uk

Beans Beans
0845 1304546 / www.beanbeans.co.uk

Burgon & Ball
01202 684141 / www.burgonandball.com

Grand Illusions
01747 854092 / www.grandillusions.com

Growing Success
01722 337744

Queenswood
01568 611281 / www.queenswood.co.uk

Secret Garden Furniture
020 8464 5327 / www.adirondack.co.uk
www.secretgardensfurniture.com

SCULPTURES AND GARDEN GAMES

118 Golf
0845 4300118 / www.118golf.co.uk

gajits biz
01386 423760 / www.shopboxuk.com

Mass N16
0207 8129700 / www.massn16.co.uk

Rawgarden
01371 870907 / www.rawgarden.com

Red Dust Ceramics
01830 540464

Silver Nutmeg
01254 820478 / www.silvernutmeg.com
www.reddustceramics.co.uk

WOOD STAIN/PAINT

Cuprinol
01753 550555 / www.cuprinol.co.uk

Hammerite
01661 830000 / www.hammerite.co.uk

PLANTS AND TURF

Amulree Exotics
01508 488101

British Field Products
01842 828266

Hidden Nursery
01565 722315

Rolawn
01904 608661 / www.rolawn.co.uk

Style Gardens
02920 598118 / www.qlawns.co.uk
www.turn-it-tropical.co.uk

PICTURE CREDITS

Alamy/58, 67/B.A.E. Inc. 109b/Jim Gibson 97/Chris Rose 78/David Stares 18; **Arcaid**/David Churchill 12b /David Mark Soulsby 41/Mark Fiennes 90a/Richard Powers 59 left; **Blustin Heath Design** 9, 10a, b, 12a, 14a, b, c, 15, 19a, 20a, b, c, 21, 27a, b, c, 29a, b, c, 30, 31, 38, 39, 41, 42a, b, 44a, b, c, 46, 48, 49a, b, 51a, b, c, 52a, b, c, 53, 54a, b, 61c, 62a, b, 63, 66, 68a, b, c, 70a, b, c, 72, 73, 74a, b, c, 81, 82a, b, c, 84a, b, c, 86a, b, c, 87b, 88, 89b, 91, 92a, b, c, 93, 94a, b, 99a, b, 100a, b, 102a, b, c, 104, 105, 106a, b, c, 110a, b, 117, 118a, b, 119, 123, 124, 127, 130a, c, 131a, 132b, 142a, 144a, b, 152c; **Lisa Buckland** 115, 118b, 125a, 128, 129, 136a, 138; **Cassell Illustrated**/Sam Bailey 8, 22, 36, 49, 56, 76, 96, 114, 134; **Corbis UK Ltd**/Gillian Darley, Edifice 83/Edifice 11a /Bob Krist 89/Philippa Lewis, Edifice 39; **Extremis/Tel: +44 (0)1483 877875** 109a; **Garden Picture Library**/Pernilla Bergdahl 141b/John Glover 148a/ James Guillam 141b/ Francois de Heel 140a/Neil Holmes 141a/Jason Ingram 140b/Clive Nichols 151/ Howard Rice 148b/Janet Sorrell 146/John Swithinbank 107a; **Imago Productions** 19b, c, 34, 65, 116, 120, 125b, 130b, 131b, 132a, 137, 144c, 152a, b; **The Interior Archive**/Fritz von Schulenburg 59a/Mark Luscombe-Whyte/Architect: Sarah Wigglesworth 87; **Andrew Lawson**/107 bottom centre; **Red Cover**/61a, 69/ Jon Bouchier 11b/Winfried Heinze 57/Graham Atkins-Hughes 65/Niall McDiarmid 61b/Robert O'Dea 7/Oscar Paisley 62b/Kim Sayer 17; **Rex Features**/Richard Gardner (RGA)

BIBLIOGRAPHY

Brickwork, Andrew Plumridge & Wim Meulenkamp, Seven Dials, 2000

Contemporary Details, Nonie Niesewand, Reed International Books Ltd, 1992

Contemporary Windows, Amanda Baillieu, Mitchell Beazley, 2003

Doors: Excellence in International Design, Gretl and Julius Hoffman, Verlag, 1977

Eco-renovations, Edward Harland, Chelsea Green Publishing Co., 1999

Glass Construction Manual, Schittich, Staib, Balkow, Schuler, Sobek, Birkhäuser Publishers for Architecture, 1999

Greener Building, Keith Hall & Peter Warm, The Green Building Press, Fourth Edition

Home Book, Oliver Heath, Cassell Illustrated, 2004

How to Make Your Garden Grow, Lisa and Toby Buckland, Cassell Illustrated, 2004

Light Construction, Terence Riley, The Museum of Modern Art, 1995

Property Ladder, Sarah Beeny, Cassell Illustrated, 2002

Suburban Style, Helena Barrett & John Phillips, Guild Publishing London, 1987

The Art of Outdoor Lighting, Randall Whitehead, Rockport Publishers, 2001

The Eco-Design Handbook, Alastair Faud-Luke, Thames & Hudson Ltd. 2002

The Elements of Style, Stephen Calloway, Mitchell Beazley, 1991

Your House: the Outside View, John Prizeman, Hutchinson & Co (Publishers) Ltd., 1975

Colour Outside, Tom Porter, Architect P, 1982

Planning Department advisory booklet

Understanding the Building Regulations, Simon Polley, E& FN Spon, 1995

INDEX

aluminium 91
Ange and Lee's Gothic house 19, 137
Areas of Outstanding Beauty 25
Art Deco 12, 13, 39, 42
Art Deco house 14, 129, 144
Art Nouveau 13, 39, 46
Arts and Crafts movement 13, 39, 46
awnings 67

balconies 69
Baroque style 13
Barry and Kerry's Mondrian house 53, 84
Beachcomber house (Nikki and Colin's) 29, 118
Bed-zed 12
Birmingham bar 47
blinds 71–3
    case study 74
    light through 73
boundaries 76, 94
    defining 16
    Party Wall agreement 25–6
    permission for 25
bricks 88–9
    laying 88
    types 89
budget 32, 40
Building Control permissions 26
building materials 33
building records 23
Building Regulations 26, 60

candles 110
Celtic garden 137
Chris's eccentric house 20, 94
Christianity 37
Christmas 37
cities 10
cladding 77, 83–91
    case studies 84, 86, 92
    for doors 42
    metal 91
    mud 87
    removing 83
    rendering 90
    roofs 93
    stone 87–8
    tiles 89

timber 85
    unusual materials 90
Claire's Fruit Machine house 74
climbers 148–9
Colonial houses (Julia and Bernadette's) 15, 137
colour 30
    in areas of UK 79
    for doors 45
    light and 99
    for walls 78–81
columns 16
community, idea of 10
concept board 18
Conservation Areas 24, 25, 59
conservatories, building regulations 60
containers 150–2
    case study 152
contractors, finding 33
contracts 33
copper 91
cottage style 21, 39
Cubism 39
curtains 71
    light through 73
    linings 73

damp 34
daylight 98–9
    light levels 58
design process 28–33
    budget 32
    colour 30
    drawings to scale 31
Diamond house 70, 129
Diwali 37
door casing 43
door frames 43
door furniture 40, 47–9
door knockers 48
door lining 43
doorbells 48
doors 16, 21, 36, 37–46
    aluminium 42
    case study 44
    colours 45
    draught excluders 40
    garage 54
    hinges 47
    individuality 43
    lighting 104
    locks 47
    materials for 41–2

painting 43
    personal preferences 37
    practical considerations 40
    recycled 46
    rituals and traditions associated with 17, 37
    security 40, 47
    size of opening 40
    steel 42
    styles 38–9
    terminology 43
    types 43
    UPVC 42
    vision panels 40, 46
    wood 41
Downing Street (No.10) 43
drainpipes 93
draught excluders 40
drawings, to scale 31
driveways 123–5
    materials for 125
    new 124
dry dash 35

eccentric house (Chris's) 20, 94
Edwardian style 12, 13, 39
Elaine's Mediterranean house 51, 137, 152
electricity, wiring for 131–2
entrances 36–55
    dos and don'ts 55
environment 16

fences 94
    altering 26
    taking out 121
fire, means of escape in 60
floodlighting 105
fountains 132
Fruit Machine house 74
furniture, outdoor 129
Futurism 39

garage doors 54
garden:
    beds and borders 138–9
    case studies 118, 130, 140
    climbers for 148–9
    containers for 150–1
        case study 152
    cosmetic changes to 122
    designing 117
    dos and don'ts 133, 153
    hard landscaping 114–33

buying materials 122
hedges 145–9
ideas for 139
inspiration 119–20
lawn 142–3
    turfing 144
planning 117, 138–9
planting 135–6
plants for 140–1
soft landscaping 134–53
starting work on 121–2
garden furniture 129
garden suburbs 10
Georgian style 11, 13, 21, 38, 50
glass:
    blocks 66
    energy-efficient 64
    float (plate) 64
    laminated 65
    obscured 64
    patterned 64
    recycled 66
    for security 47
    sheet 64
    stained 46, 65
    surface treatments 66
    textured 64
    toughened/safety 64–5
    types 64–5
    for windows 64–6
    wired 65
Gothic house 19, 137
Gothic revival 38
grants 24
guttering 93

Hampstead Garden Suburb 10
Hazel's Edward Hopper house 99,
    102, 129
heat loss, front doors and 46
hedges 145–9
    removing 121
Hinduism 37
hinges, door 47
history of house, researching 23, 24
Holt, Lolly and John 127
Hopper (Edward) house (Hazel's)
    99, 102, 129
house name 48–9
house number 48–9
    lighting 105

India 17
inspiration 28

intumescent strip 43
Italian renaissance 38
Italy 16

Jacobean style 13
Jacobethan style 12, 39
Japanese-style house 82
Jason and Kate's Rock and Roll
    house 52, 54, 94, 137
Julia and Bernadette's houses 15,
    137
Julie's Princess house 51, 68, 130

Kay's Art Deco house 14, 129, 144
King, Julie, Princess house 51, 68,
    130

landscaping:
    hard 114–33
        dos and don'ts 133
        starting work on 121–2
    soft 134–53
        dos and don'ts 153
lanterns 110
Larna's house 73, 92
lawn:
    designing 142–3
    turfing 144
lead flashing 35
leadwork 46
legislation 25–6
Letchworth 10
letterboxes 47, 48
light levels 58
light pollution 101
lighting 96–113
    accent 103
    ambient 103
    artificial 100–13
    backlighting 107
    candles and 110
    case studies 102, 106
    colour and 99
    colour-changing 109
    creating effects 108
    daylight 98–9
    design 101
    dos and don'ts 113
    effect indoors 100
    feature 107
    fittings 109
    floodlighting 105
    importance of 97
    installation 112

light layering 108
    planning schemes 111–12
    security 103
    task lighting 103, 104–5
    temporary 109–10
    types 103–10
    white light 108
    wiring for 131, 132
listed buildings 25
    restrictions 38, 59
locks:
    door 47
    window 63
Lolly's house 54
London bar 47

Mackintosh, Charles Rennie 39
Mark and Louise's house 50, 99
Mediterranean house 51, 137, 152
metals, for cladding 91
metalwork, repairing 35
mezuzah 17
Modern Movement 12, 13
Mondrian house (Barry and Kerry's)
    53, 84
'moon lighting' 108
mosaics, for steps 53
Motorbike house 21, 99, 106, 137
mud, for cladding 87

name of house 48–9
National Parks 25
nautical house 27
neighbourhood, impact on 15–17
Nepal 17
Netherlands 16
Nikki and Colin's Beachcomber
    house 29, 118
noise pollution 60
Notting Hill, London 10
number of house 48–9
    lighting 105

original features:
    doors 38, 46
    repairing 34–5
    restoring 24
    windows 59
ornamentation 10

paint, types 80
painting:
    doors 43
    styles and effects 81

walls 78–81
Party Wall agreement 26
pathways, designing 126
paving 126–7
    materials for 127
    removing 121
pebbledash 35, 90
penalties 33
Permitted Development Rights
    25–6
personality, expressing 18
planning 23–6
    steps 24
planning applications 26
planning office 24
planning permission 25
plants 140–1
    choosing 135
    climbers 148–9
    creating style with 136–7
    damage from 35
    for hedging 145–6
    for ponds 132
plastics, for glazing 66
pointing 35
pollution:
    light 101
    noise 60
ponds 131
    accessories for 132
porches 16, 25, 36, 50–1
    case study 52
    lighting 104–5
Post-Modern 13
potager 139
Princess house (Julie's) 51, 68,
    130
professional advice 24
project management 32
projections (images) 81
protected areas 25

quotes, obtaining 33

Regency style 11, 13, 50
regulations:
    Building Regulations 26, 60
    for windows 59–60
rendering 35, 90
    resembling stone 16
right to light 26
rills 131
rituals 17

Robin Hood house 86
Rock and Roll house (Jason and
    Kate's) 52, 54, 94, 137
roofs 93
Rowe, Eve, Motorbike house 21,
    99, 106, 137

safety, regulations 60
scale drawings 31
screens 128, 145
seasonal decoration 17
seating 128–9
secondary glazing 60, 62
security:
    doors 40, 47
    garden furniture 129
    lighting 103
    windows 63
servants 10
services, on façade 93
shrines 17
shutters 63, 69
slums 10
stained glass 46, 65
steel 91
stencils 81
steps 53
stone, for cladding 87–8
structural problems 34–5
stucco 16, 35, 77
style:
    for garden 136–7
    identifying 11–13
        case study 14
suburbs 10
Sunspan house 39
surface problems 34–5

task lighting 103, 104–5
tiles, as cladding 89
trees, removing 121
trompe l'oeil 81
Tudor style 13
Tune, Zoe, house 43, 44

UPVC:
    doors 42
    windows 16, 62

value of property 16
    increasing 33
ventilation, building regulations 60
verandah 15

Victoria, Queen 45
Victorian style 11, 13, 21, 38, 50
vision panels 40, 46

walls 76–95
    boundary 94
    case studies:
        cladding 84, 86, 92
        painting 82
    cladding 83–91
    dos and don'ts 95
    painting 78–81
    Party Wall agreement 25–6
    repairing 35
warping 46
water features:
    lighting 107
    wiring for 131–2
Waterfall house 129
weddings 37
window awnings 67
window boxes 67
window furniture 63
window sill 63
window surrounds 69
windows 16, 56–75
    case study 68
    coverings for 71–3
    defining 59
    dos and don'ts 75
    expressing personality 58
    frames 62
    glass for 64–6
    maintenance 63
    making decisions on 57
    motorized treatments 73
    opening 59
    orientation 58
    regulations on 59
    repairing 35
    security 63
    styles 61
    types 61–2
    UPVC 16
wood:
    cladding 85
        case study 86
    for doors 41
    expansion and shrinkage 43
    for steps 53
    for window frames 62
workmanship 33